THE
DEVIL

THE
DEVIL

AMELIA WILSON

First edition for the United States and Canada published by
Barron's Educational Series, Inc., 2002

Produced by PRC Publishing Ltd.,
64 Brewery Road, London N7 9NT
A member of **Chrysalis** Books plc

All inquiries should be addressed to:
Barron's Educational Series, Inc.
250 Wireless Boulevard
Hauppauge, NY 11788
http://www.barronseduc.com

International Standard Book No. 0-7641-5540-7

Library of Congress Catalog Card No. 2001098846

Printed and bound in Taiwan

9 8 7 6 5 4 3 2 1

The publisher wishes to thank those who kindly supplied the
illustrations and photography for this book, as follows:

Pages 1, 28 and 86-87 courtesy of The Art Archive/Museo del
Prado Madrid/Dagli Orti (A);
Pages 7, 10, 12, 16, 24, 62, 63, 72, 81, 84, 88 (top and bot-
tom), 92, 95, 99, 104, 108, 109 and 116 courtesy of ©
Bettmann/CORBIS;
Page 8 courtesy of The Art Archive/Palazzo Farnese
Caprarola/Dagli Orti;
Pages 9, 26, 110, 111 and 112-113 courtesy of © CORBIS;
Pages 11, 22, 52 and 93 courtesy of The Art Archive/Museo
Correr Venice/Dagli Orti (A);
Pages 13, 33 and 46 courtesy of © Historical Picture
Archive/CORBIS;
Pages 14, 79, 82, 83, 90, 91 and 107 courtesy of The Art
Archive/Dagli Orti (A);
Page 15 courtesy of The Art Archive/Museo del Prado
Madrid/Album/Joseph Martin;
Page 17 courtesy of © Francis G. Mayer/CORBIS;
Page 19 courtesy of The Art Archive/National Museum of
Prague/Dagli Orti;
Pages 21, 55, 66, 76 and 117 courtesy of The Art
Archive/Museo del Prado Madrid/Dagli Orti;
Pages 23, 36 and 78 courtesy of The Art Archive/The Art
Archive;
Page 25 courtesy of The Art Archive/National Museum
Damascus Syria/Dagli Orti (A);
Page 27 courtesy of The Art Archive/British Library/British
Library;
Page 31 courtesy of The Art Archive/British Museum/Eileen
Tweedy;
Page 34 courtesy of The Art Archive/Pinacoteca Nazionale
Bologna/Dagli Orti;
Pages 35 and 71courtesy of © Archivo Iconografico,
S.A./CORBIS;
Page 37 courtesy of The Art Archive/Musée Départemental
des Vosges Epinal/Dagli Orti;
Page 39 courtesy of The Art Archive/Victoria and Albert
Museum London/Graham Brandon;
Page 41 courtesy of © Elio Ciol/CORBIS;
Pages 42, 51, 97, 101 and 103 courtesy of © Chris
Hellier/CORBIS;
Pages 43 and 45 courtesy of The Art Archive/Suermondt
Museum Aachen/Dagli Orti (A);

Page 48 courtesy of The Art Archive/Scrovegni Chapel
Padua/Dagli Orti (A);
Page 49 courtesy of The Art Archive/Dagli Orti;
Pages 50 and 61 courtesy of © Araldo de Luca/CORBIS;
Pages 54, 64 and 70 courtesy of The Art Archive/Biblioteca
Nazionale Marciana Venice/Dagli Orti (A);
Page 57 courtesy of The Art Archive/Museo Arte Sacra S
Casciano Val di Pesa/Dagli Orti (A);
Page 58 courtesy of The Art Archive/Museo Civico
Correggio/Dagli Orti (A);
Page 60 courtesy of © Marc Garanger/CORBIS;
Page 65 courtesy of The Art Archive/Musée Atger
Montpellier/Dagli Orti;
Page 69 courtesy of © Arte & Immagini srl/CORBIS;
Page 73 courtesy of The Art Archive/Stadtmuseum Trier
(Salomon Collection)/Dagli Orti (A);
Page 75 courtesy of The Art Archive/Musée du Louvre
Paris/Dagli Orti (A);
Page 77, courtesy of The Art Archive/Cason del Buen Retiro
Madrid/Album/Joseph Martin;
Page 80 courtesy of The Art Archive/Victoria and Albert
Museum London/Eileen Tweedy;
Page 89 courtesy of © Ali Meyer/CORBIS;
Page 98 courtesy of The Art Archive/Musée d'Orsay
Paris/Dagli Orti;
Page 100 courtesy of The Art Archive/Bibliothèque des Arts
Décoratifs Paris/Dagli Orti;
Page 106 courtesy of The Art Archive/Palazzo Pitti
Florence/Dagli Orti (A);
Page 115 courtesy of © Paul A. Souders/CORBIS;
Page 118 courtesy of © Christel Gerstenberg/CORBIS;
Page 119 courtesy of The Kobal Collection/Paramount;
Pages 120-121 courtesy of The Kobal Collection/Warner
Bros.;
Pages 122 and 123 courtesy of The Kobal Collection/20th
Century Fox;
Page 124 courtesy of © Hulton-Deutsch Collection/CORBIS;
Page 125 courtesy of © Owen Franken/CORBIS;
Page 126 courtesy of © Macduff Everton/CORBIS;
Page 127 courtesy of © Burstein Collection/CORBIS.

The illustration on the front cover was supplied courtesy of ©
Bettmann/CORBIS.

The photograph on the back cover was supplied courtesy of
The Kobal Collection/20th Century Fox.

CONTENTS

INTRODUCTION

"O thou! whatever title suit thee,

Auld Hornie, Satan, Nick, or Clootie!"

—Robert Burns, *Address to the Devil*

Under many names and in many guises, the Devil has tempted, teased, and tricked humankind for centuries. From the familiar goat-legged, horned demon of the past, to his modern incarnation as a charmer in a good suit, the image of the Devil has remained in our midst, ably adapting to keep pace with the times. While perhaps relatively few people today believe in the Devil as an actual entity, "Old Horny" has managed to maintain his appeal as the embodiment of sin.

Down through the ages, the Devil has been depicted countless times in our folklore and legends, religious texts, art, and literature. In more recent times, he has made the leap into mass-produced popular culture such as movies, rock music, and television. His likeness has been used to frighten, instruct, amuse, and arouse us, and even to sell luncheon meat. But who exactly is this super-demon we know by so many names? How did such a powerful figure of darkness emerge, and why has his image remained so persistent in the popular imagination? Just what is it about the nefarious doings of the Devil and his wicked brood that have made them the source of such endless fascination?

The story of the Devil, as we've come to know him, is a delicious one indeed. It's a rich and complex stew of long-evolved religious and spiritual traditions absorbed from many cultures, judiciously blended, of course, with our usual favorite spices: politics, power, and sex. Here we shall take a blameless look at this long history and follow the life of the fiend from his earliest origins and possible antecedents, to his long-running role as the arch-nemesis of God and man.

Right: This depiction of a demon by Albrecht Dürer features several of the more typical attributes we have come to associate with the Devil, including hairy satyrlike legs.

The Devil

The Fall of the Rebel Angels *(detail) by Giovanni del Vecchi (1536–1615), ceiling fresco, Sala degli Angeli. This version of the battle in Heaven shows Satan's routed minions with pointed ears and animal tails and feet.*

Ideas that frequently originated in earlier cultures' beliefs and lore, mixed with the theological and political upheavals marking the history of Christianity and its rise to popularity and power helped to shape the unexpectedly scant concrete Biblical mentions into a thoroughly fleshed out conception of evil. Over time, more and more scholars, artists, and writers have added their own fantastic thoughts and speculations to the collection of "common knowledge" detailing the lore of the Devil, which helped to spread and popularize ideas (and some famous errors).

Ask the average person what things he or she knows about the Devil and you'll usually be met with a whole range of disparate notions from familiar cultural clichés to popular Christian beliefs. One of the most enduring visual portrayals we see down through the centuries is that of Satan, the fallen angel.

People familiar with the Bible might well remember some portion of the oft-illustrated account, from the book of Revelation, of the fall of the rebel angels:

> "And there was a great battle in heaven, Michael and his angels fought with the dragon, and the dragon fought and his angels: and they prevailed not, neither was their place found any more in heaven. And that great dragon was cast out, that old serpent, who is called the Devil and Satan, who seduceth the whole world; and he was cast unto the earth, and his angels were thrown down with him." (Revelation, 12:7-9)

Right: The noble Christian knight of Albrecht Dürer's 1513 famous copper-plate engraving The Knight, Death, and The Devil *is able to pass by Death and the Devil because of his steadfast faith.*

While the rest of us might have a little hazier recall on the more precise details of Satan's origins, we are all certainly familiar with Hell, where, along with his legions of lesser followers, the Devil has been consigned.

This once revered and holy creature, an angel of the Lord now brought low, retains his wings in many popular depictions—although they often more closely resemble those of a bat than the feathers of a Heavenly angel. Satan is frequently shown as being either red or black in color, the average daily temperature in Hell presumably being somewhat higher than it is on the Earth's surface. He is generally depicted as being monstrous, befitting his fallen status, with attributes taken from animals and non-Christian (and therefore unholy) mythological creatures.

The basic body model for the Devil in his most common incarnation seems to have been the satyr—the famously libidinous half-man, half-goat creature of classical myth, who had features such as horns, cloven hooves, and shaggy bent legs. The part-eagle, part-lion griffin and multiheaded hydra were other popular fantastical inspirations. Bits and pieces of more earthly animals appeared frequently on images of the Devil as well, including attributes pulled from snakes, dogs, and scorpions. A pitchfork or trident became a common accessory—a symbol of mastery borrowed from the Greek sea god Poseidon. The opera cape and fastidiously groomed facial hair, which might also come to mind when one thinks of the Devil, are later additions, dating from Satan's portrayal as a Romantic antihero in the nineteenth century.

Aside from the variety of physical traits that have come to represent the image of the Devil, there is

Above: Luca Signorelli (c.1441-1523) fresco depicting Hell, Orvieto Cathedral. Here the damned are crowded together where they are set upon, bitten, and beaten by winged, horned demons.

The Devil

also confusion about the origin of his name. The word "devil" is a translation of the Greek *diabolos*, which means adversary or obstructer. The term "satan," derived from the ancient Hebrew *sathane*, has a similar meaning.

As we shall see later, it was not until the books of the New Testament that Satan (or the Devil) became a proper noun, and began referring to the one specific entity that we now associate exclusively with that name. But what of all these other monikers, both scriptural and traditional, that the Devil has gone by through the centuries? You can find dozens of names and euphemisms, ranging from imposing titles such as Angel of the Abyss, Prince of Darkness, or the Archfiend, to oddly endearing nicknames such as Old Bendy, Nick, or Old Scratch, which gives the idea of an old friend rather than an embodiment of the purest evil.

There are terms frequently used for the Devil, which actually originally referred to someone (or something) else entirely: Beelzebub, Lucifer, and Mephistopheles to mention just a few. Misconceptions and mistaken identities abound and there are many that might say that's the way the Devil intends it.

Beyond the question of who Satan is, there's also the question of why he is. What role, what purpose, has the existence of this supremely evil entity served that it has enjoyed such a richly imagined and long-lasting life?

We humans have always lived at the mercy of forces and events that have seemed beyond our control: sickness and misfortune, plague, fire, earthquakes, floods, darkness at night. There are things that amaze and frighten us—not only in the incomprehensible vastness of nature, but also within ourselves: The bad

Above: The Devil card from a Tarot deck, Venice, seventeenth century, is a classic interpretation of the Devil with bat-like wings, goatish horns and beard, and animal feet. The trident, borrowed from the Greek god Poseidon is a symbol of mastery.

behavior of our fellow men and bad behavior we feel tempted to get away with. We have grand, sweeping, answerless questions: Where do we come from? Why are we here? What becomes of us after we die?

For as long as human beings have been in existence, we have tried to answer these questions for ourselves and sought ways to understand these powerful forces that surround us and affect us. Anthropologists posit that one of the reasons religion has had and maintained such a central position of importance in human cultures is because of the role it plays in helping us to formulate and think about those knotty, big questions that have confounded us for all time.

> "[Religion's] single function is to give man access to the powers which seem to control his destiny, and its single purpose is to induce those powers to be friendly to him."
> H.L. Mencken, *Treatise on the Gods*

Now, while some might find Mencken's attitude here toward one of the most powerful guiding forces of human behavior to be somewhat glib, it does at least recognize one of the traditional ways humankind has tried to use religion. Not only have people performed rituals and worshipped as a means to appreciate mysterious powers, but there is also a long legacy of attempts to influence, appease, and/or harness these

Above: Woodcut showing Lucifer and his demons guarding the mouth of Hell. The application of the name Lucifer to the Devil is widely thought to have been the result of a translation error by early Christian scholars.

powers to serve the supplicant's desires. While for most religious people those desires will take the positive form of, say, prayers for the swift recovery of the sick, there is also a long history of greedy and desperate individuals who have been willing to bargain with less reputable powers to benefit individual good fortunes. The so-called Faustian bargain, or devil's pact, became a popular theme in literature and folklore and during the witch-hunting craze in fifteenth through seventeenth century Europe. Accusations of dealings with Satan were used as a powerful political tool for intimidation and social control.

Almost every culture has its conceptions of good and evil, right and wrong, codes of morality and proper behavior, and these systems are often at least partially governed within the bounds of a religion. The presence of supernatural beings of various kinds, such as gods, demons, and spirits, which represent the entire range of traits humans can imagine, are a common element of belief in many religions around the world. Classical mythology, most pagan traditions, Zoroastrianism, Islam, Hinduism, and Judaism all contain some acknowledgement of gods or spirits, entities who are outside and above human beings in power.

Above: Illustration plate from an English philosophy book depicting Heaven and Hell. Angelic musicians strum lutes and harps among the clouds, while bat-winged, part-snake horned demons coil below the hills.

Illustration of the ritual kiss of the Sabbat from Compendium Malleficarum, *1626, by Francesco Guazzo. Thought to be a standard ceremonial practice: witches and sorcerers line up to kiss Satan's anus.*

But the development and maturity of a great and purely evil adversary in the Christian doctrine offers an unusually visible icon. Another distinguishing feature of the Christian Satan is that his role extends far beyond the merely symbolic. He is conceived as an active force for evil. This particularly dastardly demon goes out of his way to tempt, seduce, and deceive not only the wicked, but the simply unwitting.

The Devil then, as his powers and tactics evolved over the course of Western history, becomes both cause and explanation for the existence of evil, greed, lust, deceit, and general bad behavior. As the personification of sin, he also comes to be associated with all the Commandment-breaking sensual pleasures of human indulgence and desire that Christianity preached against. In other words, the Devil and his cohorts offer an irresistibly tantalizing glimpse of the forbidden.

Thus, the accounts of witch trials from the height of the witch-hunt hysteria include meticulous court reports that catalog in lurid detail the goings on at Sabbats, the ritual ceremonies where participants allegedly took part in wild dances and sex orgies featuring sodomy, homosexuality, and "crimes against nature."

The wages of sin become amply illustrated in works such as Dutch painter Hieronymus Bosch's *The Garden of Earthly Delights*, where the revelers in flesh and fruit occupying the center of the famous triptych, give way to elaborate and sadistically appropriate tortures visited upon the sinners once they reach the Hellish right panel.

As the centuries have passed since the dawn and spread of Christianity, the nature and experience of religion for the average person has undergone radical change. In the wake of the scientific, economic, and

Right: The Garden of Earthly Delights *(center panel of triptych) by Hieronymus Bosch (1450–1516). Carefree revelers frolic and indulge all the sensual pleasures of the flesh.*

political revolutions that have transformed Western culture from ancient to modern times, the place and meaning of religion in the popular mind has gradually moved from the extreme literalism of medieval belief, to the more figurative and philosophical constructs of today.

Hand in hand with the faith that created him, the Devil and what he stands for has also radically changed. It seems the more abstract modern interpretation of evil has left Old Cloots in a bit of a cultural lurch. Somehow, it seems almost insulting for what was once such a powerful and compelling figure to be reduced to his current role of movie villain and commercial pitchman.

The Garden of Earthly Delights *(detail of right panel of triptych) by Hieronymus Bosch (1450–1516). In one of the most famous depictions of Hell, the damned suffer fantastic and elaborate torture.*

But whatever one's take on the religious and moral issues surrounding Satan, the contribution his existence has lent to the art, literature, and folklore of Western culture is undeniable. That even the most rational-minded and jaded modern viewer can instantly identify and decode layers of meaning from a quick glance at the familiar silhouette attests to the enduring power of that heritage. It is time, then, to offer Old Horny a nod of recognition for the rich artistic and cultural legacy he has inspired and hope that this fantastic and enduring history will serve in some small way to give the Devil his due.

Left: Diabolus Vulgaris. Another typical depiction of a demon, this one with elongated, pointed ears, horns, and tail. It was common to color the Devil and other demons scorched black or red.

CHAPTER ONE:

Paving the Way—The Devil's Earliest Origins

BELIEFS OF ANCIENT PEOPLES

Before diving headlong into where exactly the Devil fits within the context of the Christian Bible, it would probably be helpful to lay a brief historical and cultural framework to help understand the mindset and philosophies of the ancient world. We can find several marked resemblances, as well as obvious differences, in some of the ways in which humans have attempted to address our basic philosophical and spiritual questions.

The Christian tradition that produced Satan was not developed in a vacuum. Christianity contains—as is generally true for the social institutions of all cultures—echoes, similarities, and allusions to the ways and ideas of its predecessors, neighbors, and sworn enemies. Certainly the determination of these similarities and parallels have actually been "borrowed" from other sources and which ones simply emerge in multiple cultures as a matter of independently generated coincidence will largely remain a matter of scholarly conjecture. However, in examining the belief systems of some of the other ancient peoples of the world, we begin to meet a surprisingly familiar cast of characters and events. As well as helping to create a context for the emergence of the Devil, this survey might also help us to recognize some of the ways in which our religious and cultural symbols evolve and adapt to suit the specific needs and agendas of a society.

Right: Adam and Eve *by Lucas Cranach the elder (1472–1553). Many stories in the book of Genesis share similarities with Sumerian mythology, including the creation myth and the great flood.*

THE SUMERIANS AND BABYLONIANS

To the Hebrews of the Old Testament, the Sumerian/Babylonian cultures occupied all three categories of predecessor, neighbor, and enemy. The Sumerians lived in a collection of agrarian settlements bound by the Tigris and Euphrates rivers, the fertile lands in the region now part of southern Iraq, beginning around 5000 B.C. While there is some archaeological evidence pointing to an earlier settlement date for the city of Jericho, and some data from Egypt may also predate Sumer, it is the farm-based Sumerians who provide us with the first truly complex society for which we have good information.

Before being absorbed by the rising Babylonian empire around 2000 B.C., Sumer enjoyed a long and frequently prosperous history. More than just farmers, the Sumerians were the settlers of the great ancient city-states of Kish and Ur and architects of the ziggurats—huge, square step-pyramids (the one at Ur reaching sixty feet in height), which it is believed were used by priests for celestial observation. The Sumerians established well-traveled trade routes, sailing their ships up and down the Euphrates River. They developed cuneiform—the first written language—had the earliest known written business records, a code of law, and perhaps most lastingly, they created a religion that influenced other systems of belief that sprang up later throughout the region. This included most obviously the Babylonian religion, which adopted many of the Sumerian gods and traditions wholesale. But the Sumerian legacy also made its mark on Judaism and Christianity with noticeable parallels between certain aspects of Sumerian myth and similar stories and events (such as the great flood), which are also described in the book of Genesis.

The Sumerian (and later, Babylonian) pantheon is vast and complicated, with hundreds of deities and many levels of gods and demigods, including the great warrior hero Gilgamesh. But the creation myth of the Sumerians is a very familiar sounding tale. By their account, the world is formed out of a watery abyss called abzu, or the primeval sea. This abyss was separated into Heaven (an) and Earth (ki).

The Biblical and Sumerian descriptions of the creation of man also have some striking similarities. Genesis 2:7 describes God's creation of Adam:

The Devil

"Then the LORD God formed man of dust from the ground, and breathed into his nostrils the breath of life; and man became a living being."

In the Sumerian version, the gods Enki, lord of the abzu, along with Ninhursag (another name for Ki), the Earth goddess, "kneed the 'heart' of the clay that is over the abzu" in order to "give it form"—that form being man. However, unlike God's relatively simple and successful formation of Adam, the more quar-relsome Sumerian deities have a bit more trouble with their task. Prior to getting down to business, the Sumerian gods drink too much at a feast and botch their first attempts at mak-ing their clay men. After creating several malformed versions, including one who cannot eat, they proceed to criticize one another's imperfect efforts.

More parallels between Sumerian myth and the book of Genesis can be found when we compare the Biblical paradise of Eden with the similarly beautiful Sumerian Dilmun, a pure land blessed by the god Enki and filled with sweet water, palms, and fruit trees. Genesis, which describes Eden as lying "in the east," even specifically mentions four rivers flowing out it—"And the name of the third river is Tigris, which flows east of Assyria. And the fourth river is the Euphrates." (Genesis, 2:14) By Genesis's own internal reference, Eden is geographically placed within the cradle of Sumerian civilization.

Above: The Temptation of Eve from The Haywain *(detail) by Hieronymus Bosch. Eden bears many similarities to the Sumerian garden of Dilmun. The serpent in the tree may also derive from Sumerian myth.*

Resemblances to the Eden story continue with the Sumerian myth of "Gilgamesh, Enkidu, and the Underworld," which mentions a special tree, the huluppu tree, which Inanna (goddess of love, war, and fertility, later called the more familiar name Ishtar by the Babylonians) has planted in her garden in Uruk. There, in her newly acquired huluppu, Inanna finds much to her dislike that, "a serpent who could not be charmed made its nest in the roots of the tree."

This serpent may well be a predecessor to that much more notorious serpent who tempts Eve to taste the fruit of Eden's tree of the Knowledge of Good and Evil. As we shall see, that same serpent will come to have a very strong association with the Devil in the Christian tradition, with some even asserting that the serpent in Eden is the Devil, having taken on one of his many deceitful guises.

While on the subject of serpents, it is interesting to note that the Babylonian pantheon includes the old and powerful goddess Tiamat, the primeval spirit, the "bearer of the skies and the earth"—who is customarily ascribed the attributes of a serpent or a dragon. In addition,

Above: The traditions of many ancient peoples feature strange mythological beasts that resemble the demons in this Apocalypse engraving by Albrecht Dürer. Parts of several animals were often combined to create a fantastic new creature.

when Tiamat went to war to defend the regime
of the old gods against the younger group of gods
led by Marduk (who we will meet later on as Bel-
Marduk, better known by the Canaanite name
Baal), among the forces she rallied to her side
were a horned serpent, a mushussu-dragon, and
several varieties of demon, including some gallu-
demons, which were capable of assuming
different forms.

The Babylonian tradition features many such
fantastical demons and monsters, including the
Bull of Heaven (another creature with horns),
which was created for the specific purpose of
defeating the great warrior demigod Gilgamesh.
The Bull of Heaven hurls spittle and excrement
at Gilgamesh in battle, and with a snorting blast,
opens a hole large enough to entrap 200 men in
the Earth.

Other Babylonian monsters contained features of several different creatures combined—a common
pattern followed by many later depictions of Satan. The description given of Anzu, a guardian beast,
sounds not terribly dissimilar from that of a griffin. Anzu had the face and paws of a lion, and eagle
talons and wings. Another creature that will eventually have Satanic associations is the scorpion, and
here too, the Babylonians provide a representative in their cadre of monsters. The aqrabuamelu are scorpi-
on-men, fearsome creatures whose "glance is death." Not specifically described as being evil, the
aqrabuamelu served as the guardians of the gate to the underworld known as Kurnugi.

Above: Dragon from an illustration for Dante's Divine Comedy *by Gustave Dore. Dragons and serpents are
two of the most enduring and common mythological creatures in the ancient world. The old Sumerian goddess
Tiamat was often associated with either a dragon or serpent.*

The conception of the underworld in the Babylonian faith is drawn from the tradition already set out by their Sumerian predecessors. The name for the Babylonian underworld, Kurnugi, actually comes from the Sumerian term for "land of no return." Taken in its totality, Kurnugi appears to have more in common with the Hades of classical myth than it does with Christian Hell. But there are some interesting similarities.

One of the epic Gilgamesh legends recounts a temporary visit to Kurnugi made by Gilgamesh's great friend Enkidu. One could make such a round-trip passage while still alive, so long as all of the proper rules of etiquette were observed. Upon Enkidu's return, Gilgamesh asks his friend to give a report of his journey, and while giving Gilgamesh his observances of the dead who were in Kurnugi, Enkidu mentions that there were some dead who were cared for, and some who were not. There are other indications that not all the dead were regarded as equals in Kurnugi. Certain individuals, such as priests and heroes, seem to have been selected to reside in the house of Ereshkigal, the ruling goddess of Kurnugi. However, in the house of her consort, Nergal, the situation is considerably bleaker. The residents in Nergal's house live in darkness, breathe dust, wear rags, and eat mud.

Underworld queen ruler Ereshkigal has a messenger named Namtar, who is also called the Fate-Cutter and herald of death. More than a mere courier for Ereshkigal, Namtar has a special power of his own—the control of sixty diseases affecting all the various parts of the human body. Direct offerings to

The Devil

Namtar were thought to help avoid illness. The description of Namtar and the role he plays as both messenger, and herald of death, bears a likeness to the figure of Hermes Psychopompos, the Guide of Souls from classical Greek mythology.

The Babylonian god Marduk, who emerges as the leader of the pantheon following his defeat of the forces of serpent-associated primeval goddess Tiamat, also went by the name Bel and the two were often combined as Bel-Marduk. In the Babylonian tradition, Marduk was a powerful and proud warrior god, who brought the cataclysm of the great flood, but he was not portrayed as a particularly vengeful figure. In one story, Marduk is challenged by the underworld god Nergal for apparent complacency in the running of his kingdom. Nergal suggests to Marduk that another flood might be in order, but Marduk responds that he has already been responsible for the deaths of most of the people on Earth and he has no plan to repeat the action. The Bel appellation for this god means "lord" and, under that name, he is regarded as the wisest of all the gods.

THE CANAANITES

The diety known to the Babylonians as Bel-Marduk went by the more Biblically familiar name Baal to the Canaanites—the people who occupied the area that used to be known as Palestine, and includes modern Israel, Syria, and Lebanon. The Greek

Above: Statuette of Baal. Bronze and gold 1400–1200 B.C. Baal, who also went by the names Bel-Marduk and Marduk, was a major god in the Sumerian, Babylonian, and Canaanite religions. A variation of his name became Beelzebub.

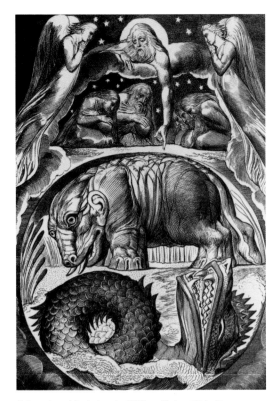

Behemoth and Leviathan by William Blake, 1825. One of warrior god Baal's great accomplishments is the slaying of the great beast Lotan—the Canaanite name for the beast Hebrew myth calls Leviathan.

term for the Canaanites—the Phoenicians—is usually reserved by historians and archaeologists to refer to this culture only after it passed from the Bronze to the Iron age, with a cutoff date generally agreed to be in the neighborhood of 1000 B.C.

The Canaanites did not leave us with as rich a legacy of archaeological information as the Sumerian/Babylonian civilizations. Unlike the Sumerians, who painstakingly chipped their cuneiform records into long-lasting stone, the Canaanites kept their accounts on perishable papyrus, most of which has been lost to the ravages of time. What we do know of the Canaanite civilization and culture was derived largely from the Bible and some secondhand Greek accounts, until the unearthing of the buried city-state of Ugarit in 1928, which provided scholars with some more reliable primary sources of information.

Early in their history, the Canaanites were held under domination by their frequent trading partner, the Egyptians. But between 2000–1000 B.C., the Canaanites came into their own as a culture, establishing the powerful city-states of Tyre and Sidon and eventually branching out to found colonies—the best known and most successful of which is Carthage. Until the defeat of Tyre and Sidon by the expanding Assyrians (complete by 572 B.C. under the famed Nebuchadnezar), the Canaanite civilization was one of the most important and influential in the region.

The Canaanite religion, like the Sumerian/Babylonian faith, contains stories that parallel certain events and ideas that turn up in the later Christian tradition. Some of the most interesting stories, for the

Right: The Jaws of Hell with the Damned, from Psalter of Henry of Blois, c.1200. The mouth, or jaws of Hell were frequently depicted literally. The Canaanite god of the underworld, Mot, was renowned for his cosmic-sized jaws, which become a euphemism for death.

purposes of exploring a context for the origins of the Devil, are the ones that tell of the battles between Baal and his two main rivals Yam and Mot.

Baal (who is, as mentioned previously, the Canaanite incarnation of the diety known to the Sumerian/Babylonian religion as the hero/warrior god Bel-Marduk) emerges as the preeminent god in the Canaanite pantheon. He is the god of fertility, thunder, and lightning ("rider of the clouds"), and is the mightiest of warriors. Among his achievements as a warrior is the slaying of the great beast Lotan, a creature who reappears as Leviathan in the Hebrew tradition. Baal is also known as a "prince" or "lord of earth"—a title later given to Satan in the New Testament.

Yam, the first of Baal's great rivals, is the god of sea and rivers who lives in a palace under the Earth. The favorite of El, the father of all Canaanite gods, Yam was chosen for kingship. But once in power, Yam acts rather like a spoiled child, threatening great destruction until he is assured that he is "beloved of El." Coming into conflict with his rival Baal, Yam is stricken down

Above: Saturn Devouring his Children *by Goya (1746–1828). The eating or sacrifice of children is a horrific practice which humans have a long history of ascribing to enemies they are attempting to vilify.*

and his body scattered. Like the Canaanite god Yam, Satan is often portrayed as having been beloved by the father of all—God—in Christianity.

The other major figure Baal comes into conflict with is Mot, also commonly known as Shar—the god of death and the underworld. Mot is described as possessing a remarkable set of jaws, mention of which becomes a euphemism for death. The jaws of Mot offer us a possible influence on the depiction of the literal "mouth" of Christian Hell. Another favorite of El and rival of Baal, Mot's conflicts with other gods result in prolonged famine and the threatened destruction of humankind.

The available accounts do not seem to offer a clear picture of the actual underworld of the Canaanite religion. On the one hand, we get the following description of Mot's ruling seat in the underworld city of Miry: "a pit is the throne on which he sits, filth the land of his heritage." Conversely, the underworld is also known as "the place of freedom," with the favored dead going to dine with Baal.

The last deity attributed to the Canaanite tradition that we are going to consider here is the somewhat mysterious Molech, or Moloch. He is described in several places in the Old Testament. Not satisfied with the customary offerings of burnt animal flesh, Molech apparently demanded that his followers sacrifice their own children to him in their worship.

A reference to this practice of sacrificing children occurs in the Old Testament book of 2 Kings, when God is instructing the Hebrew King Josiah to clean up and eradicate foreign deity worship by his people. Among a list of other tasks, including the removal of Baal idols from the temples, came the report of this met demand:

> "And he defiled Topheth, which is in the valley of the sons of Hinnom, that no one might
> burn his son or his daughter as an offering to Molech." (2 Kings, 23:10)

Later, during the accounts of witch trials in Europe during the 1500 to 1700s, a common charge leveled against those accused of witchcraft was the worship of Satan by the ritual sacrifice of children.

Since Molech does not actually appear in the primary source material unearthed at Ugarit, there is no direct mention of him in the Canaanite record. Scholars have only had the secondary references to this monstrous deity to go by, making it difficult to get an accurate read on whom this god actually represents.

One other theory holds that as the name Molech means "king"—the references might well be generic rather than specific, describing any worship of foreign gods, with the fearsome child-sacrifice thrown in to vilify the practices of these non-Jewish faiths. As frequently occurred with any deity that belonged to one of the non Judeo-Christian religions, Molech is also sometimes referred to as a demon.

The Sumerian, Babylonian, and Canaanite belief systems all have some interesting things in common with the stories and events that make up the Jewish and later Christian scriptures. However, the ancient religion that had the biggest traceable impact on the Judeo-Christian tradition is Zoroastrianism.

ZOROASTRIANISM

Among the features of Judaism, and later Christianity, that are prefigured in Zoroastrianism we find: belief in one supreme god, the existence of a powerful evil spirit who opposes the supreme god, man's free will to choose good or evil, and the prophecy of a savior who shall appear in the world and raise the dead for a final judgment. In the view of many scholars, much of what both Judaism and Christianity eventually became were drawn directly from Zoroastrian teachings.

Zoroastrianism is widely considered to be the first monotheistic religion, and this focus on one god represents a radical departure from the complicated hierarchical pantheons of the religious systems of other civilizations we have already looked at. The Persians during founding prophet Zarathustra's time similarly worshipped many deities. When he began preaching his monotheistic views, Zarathustra was initially attacked for his teaching. Eventually, however, his teachings were accepted by the king and Zoroastrianism became the state religion of Persia. Both Cyrus and Darius, two of the greatest Persian rulers, were followers. When Arabs invaded and overran Persia in 650 B.C., a small band of Zoroastrians fled to India where most are concentrated today. Although the number of modern Zoroastrians is small, numbering perhaps 140,000 followers, it remains one of the oldest religions that is still in current practice.

Zoroastrianism was founded by Zarathustra (Zoroaster in Greek) probably somewhere between 1400 and 1000 B.C. Zarathustra was living as a hermit on a mountain in Persia (now Iran), when he received a visit from the god Ahura Mazda. Ahura Mazda proclaimed himself to Zarathustra as the one god in the universe. Believing that he had been entrusted with vital information, Zarathustra set down the

Gathas, seventeen poetic hymns that form the most sacred section of the Zoroastrian scripture, the Avesta.

Ahura Mazda ("Wise Lord") is portrayed as all good and the creator of all good things including the Earth and man. Ahura Mazda's opponent, Anghra Mainyu, is not usually depicted as a god, but most commonly described as a sort of spirit—and the embodiment and creator of all that is evil. This concentration of all evil in one entity, and no other aspects to balance it, is something quite different from the more multifaceted deities of the polytheistic religions of the region.

Humankind is also given responsibility to care for that which has been given him:

> "When Ahura Mazda the Lord first created humanity, He gave the following order: 'Be diligent to save your souls; I shall then provide for your bodily matters. For it is impossible to save your souls without you.'" (Dk6.291, tr. Shaked)

After death, souls are judged at the Bridge of the Separator, where reward or punishment is given based on how righteously the deceased had spent their time on Earth. Those souls found to be worthy, ascended to the abode of joy and light, while the wicked descended into Hell.

There is also mention in Zoroastrian writings of the Saoshyant, or savior, who will appear in the world, and herald the coming of a final cosmic battle that will mark the ultimate triumph of good over evil (the defeat of Anghra Mainyu, the spirit of evil.) The Saoshyant, like Jesus Christ, will also preside over a final judgment of the dead.

Above: The Lord Answering Job out of the Whirlwind by William Blake. Depictions of God are permitted in the Christian tradition, but other monotheistic religions, Judaism, Islam, and Zoroastrianism do not allow it.

CHAPTER TWO:

Becoming Satan—The Devil in the Bible

Now that we have looked at what some of the other major ancient religions of the Near East thought about the place of gods, monsters, spirits, and the afterlife, it is time to turn our attention to the religious tradition that gave rise to the form of Satan as we have come to know him.

Considering the prominent place Satan came to occupy in the Christian faith, it seems a reasonable enough expectation that the entire Bible would be littered with references to our famous Prince of Darkness. While there are indeed mentions of Satan in the Hebrew Bible (the Tanakh, or what Christians refer to as the Old Testament, which is comprised of the thirty-nine books of scripture accepted by both Jews and Christians) his elevation to a specific entity—and a specifically evil entity—appears to be a Christian concept alone. As we shall see later, it was early Christian scholars, translators, and promoters such as Origen and St. Jerome, combing back through the Hebrew scripture looking for earlier evidence of Satan, who interpreted several scriptural passages in a way that lined up with their beliefs.

THE HEBREW BIBLE

> "I am the LORD your God, who brought you out of the land of Egypt, out of the house
> of bondage. You shall have no other gods before me." (Exodus 20:2-3)

The history of the Hebrew people, which we generally think of as the Jewish nation, really begins with Abraham, who led a group of nomads from an area near the Babylonian city-state of Ur into Palestine

Right: Mid seventeenth-century print depicting the suffering of Job. The image of Satan, here depicted with wings and a serpent tail, undergoes dramatic changes between the Hebrew Bible and the New Testament.

around 1800 B.C. A drought pushed these nomadic herders into Egypt, where they lived for several decades under harsh persecution. It was during the departure from Egypt around 1270 B.C., which is recounted in the book of Exodus, that Moses received the Ten Commandments from the god Yaweh.

Yaweh seems to have his origination in the Sumerian/Babylonian tradition. It is following the handing down of the Ten Commandments that the Hebrews exclusive belief in one almighty God was truly solidified. This acceptance of a single deity was a clear break from the religious traditions of their neighbors in Babylon and Canaan—a similar break to that which happened in Persia, which also made the switch from a traditional polytheistic system to a monotheistic one following the teaching of Zarathrustra.

There are many accounts in the Old Testament of the Jews self-policing their one-god policy, by clearing statues of Baal and other gods of neighboring civilizations out of temples and by other actions. Although, considering how often the region the Hebrews called home was conquered and influenced by various empires, it hardly seems surprising that a portion of the populous would have a difficult time knowing which god they were supposed to be pledging their loyalty to. One way the Hebrews sought to control

Above: Heaven and Hell *(detail), from Church of St. Petronius, Bologna, Italy, fifteenth century. Demons in the Hebrew Bible were often actually vilified gods of foreign religions who were seen as competition to Yaweh.*

The Devil

this influence of polytheistic religious habits was by demonizing the gods of these other religions.

> "They sacrificed to demons, which are not God—gods they had not known, gods that recently appeared, gods your fathers did not fear." (Deuteronomy 32:17)

As we discussed in the last chapter, this process of demonizing may well be the origin of Molech's terrifying habit of demanding the sacrifice of children. Another likely case of a demonized foreign god is Beelzebub.

Many scholars believe that the name Beelzebub is simply a corrupted translation of a variation on the Canaanite god Baal's name. In this case, the name Baal-Zebul which meant "prince Baal" or "Baal, Lord of the House"— got changed to Baal-Zebub, which translated to the far more demonic sounding "Lord of the Flies." There is disagreement though, as to whether this was an innocent translation error, or if the misnaming was a deliberate demonization of an extremely popular foreign god.

But there are other sources of demons and evil spirits in the Hebrew tradition. Mental distress was frequently thought to be the result of an outside influence:

Above: The Devil Joins Them *by Goya, nineteenth century. Evil spirits, always sent by God himself in the Hebrew Bible, were cited as the cause of mental distress and disorder.*

"And on the morrow an evil spirit from God rushed upon Saul, and he raved within his house, while David was playing the lyre, as he did day by day. Saul had his spear in his hand." (1 Samuel 18:10)

But here, as elsewhere within the Hebrew Bible, the evil spirit causing this distress was sent directly by God himself. Outside of the Tanakh books proper—in spite of the prohibitions against it—belief in demons and spirits seems to have been fairly commonplace, and ancient Hebrew folklore as well as some Talmudic texts contain references to creatures such as Lilith, the legendary female demon who probably originated in Sumerian myth. Lilith's initial association was as a threat to childbirth, but later Medieval folktales created an origin story for her, casting her as Adam's first wife, before Eve was created. In this later folklore, Lilith refused to be sexually submissive to Adam, so she left Eden and was replaced with the more subservient Eve. Outside of Eden, Lilith reportedly turned to her baby-stealing ways.

Monsters have their place in the Hebrew tradition as well, the most well-known being the twosome of Behemoth and Leviathan, the great beasts of land and water who both make appearances in the book of Job. As far as the Old Testament goes, both of these beasts seem mostly remarkable for being wild creatures of immense size rather than being evil. So, with the exception of a few demonized foreign gods, and the occasional God-dispatched evil spirit, the Hebrew Bible is relatively free of genuine malevolent supernatural entities.

Above: Behemoth from Collin de Phlancy's Dictionnaire Infernal, *Paris 1863. Monstrous beasts such as Behemoth (here depicted as a huge-bellied elephant) were a longstanding fixture in Hebrew lore.*

But if demons and evil spirits play such a small role in the Hebrew Bible, where is the most evil spirit of them all? What of Satan? He does show up in the Tanakh—in fact, isn't he the one who rained down all that torment on poor Job?

ENTER SATAN

The word "devil" is nowhere to be found in the Hebrew Bible. This is because the derivation of devil is Greek—from *diabolos,* meaning adversary. Greek is the language of the New Testament, the books of which did not even begin to be written until generations after the death of Jesus Christ. The Tanakh, or Old Testament, was written in Hebrew, where the word with the best equivalent meaning to "devil" is "satan." The definitions of the two words are similar but the meanings they assumed in the Hebrew Old Testament and the Christian New Testament are quite different, indeed.

The word "satan" is used in two different ways in the Hebrew Bible. They are both related, but neither refers to the specifically evil entity we have come to know as Satan or the Devil in the Christian faith.

The most common use is as a generic reference to anything or anyone that acts as an adversary or obstacle. In the story of Balaam's ass, for example, we read:

Above: Leprous Job Visited by his Wife, *Georges de la Tour (1593–1652). The story of faithful Job's testing by God is an example of an allegorical story told in the ancient Hebrew tradition of Aggadic literature.*

"So Balaam rose in the morning, and saddled his ass, and went with the princes of Moab. But God's anger was kindled because he went; and the angel of the LORD took his stand in the way as an adversary." (Numbers 22:21-22)

If we read this passage with the original Hebrew term in place, "as an adversary" becomes "as a satan." The second use does actually refer to a definite being. This use of Satan (and most translations of the Bible will capitalize the name as a proper noun in these passages) stems from the Hebrew *ha'satan*, which means "the adversary."

In the story of Job, Satan does refer to a definite character, playing the Adversary as a member of God's sort of court or council. It is probably the best-known use of Satan in the Old Testament. But is the Satan portrayed in Job the same evil Satan of the Christian tradition?

When God holds up Job as an example of a good and worthy man, Satan offers the opinion that Job's uprightness is the result of his good fortune and that if a string of bad luck should befall him, he would instead curse God:

"Now there was a day when the sons of God came to present themselves before the LORD, and Satan also came among them. The LORD said to Satan, 'Whence have you come?' Satan answered the LORD, 'From going to and fro on the earth, and from walking up and down on it.'

"And the LORD said to Satan, 'Have you considered my servant Job, that there is none like him on the earth, a blameless and upright man, who fears God and turns away from evil?'

"Then Satan answered the LORD, 'Does Job fear God for nought? Hast thou not put a hedge about him and his house and all that he has, on every side? Thou hast blessed the work of his hands, and his possessions have increased in the land. But put forth thy hand now, and touch all that he has, and he will curse thee to thy face.'

"And the LORD said to Satan, 'Behold, all that he has is in your power; only upon himself do not put forth your hand.' So Satan went forth from the presence of the LORD."
(Job 1:6–12)

Most people who are familiar with this famous story, but haven't actually read the scripture in some time, remember correctly that Satan is the one who actually performs the destructive acts against Job. What most people don't recall is that he does so only under God's instruction. When Job withstands the initial set of trials and maintains his faith, God is the one who instructs Satan to turn up the pressure on Job, inflicting greater, physical misfortune by causing boils and other personal injury.

The Satan in the story of Job is really a device in a traditional Jewish allegorical tale—Aggadah—used to illustrate a concept. Such aggadic stories abound in Talmudic literature and the frequent parables told by Jesus to his followers are in the same tradition. The Satan in Job, then, is filling the role of the Adversary,

Above: Satan by William Blake (1757–1827). The role of Satan as an individual in the Old Testament is closer to that of an agent provocateur than that of a truly evil entity.

the one who God has appointed to question the way of things. His role is necessary to advance the point of the story—that the reasons why even righteous people sometimes suffer are not the province of man's limited understanding, but are known to God alone. While some might view his "testing" of Job as excessive, Satan is still acting only within the parameters set for him by God, at God's instruction. If Satan can be described as evil in the story of Job, it is only at God's behest.

Another example of the name Satan being used to denote a specific individual occurs in the book of Zechariah. Here we have a confrontation between two groups of Jews. One group, Joshua's group, represents those who have returned from the exile imposed upon them by the old Babylonian regime. The new foreign government, the Persians, under their religiously tolerant Zoroastrian King Cyrus, encouraged the exiled Jews to return to their homeland to rebuild their great temple in Jerusalem.

Many of those exiled had been sent away by the Babylonians because they were influential and educated individuals and were seen as potential troublemakers. Upon their return, these former exiles met resistance from those Jews, who had remained in the area. They did not want to relinquish the power and positions they had been able to assume in the sudden absence of their traditional societal leaders.

The prophet Zechariah, our narrator in this tale, is on the side of the returning group—led by Joshua—that wishes to rebuild the temple:

> "And he showed me Joshua the high priest standing before the angel of the LORD, and Satan standing at his right hand to thwart him. And the LORD said to Satan, 'The LORD rebukes you, O Satan; the LORD that has chosen Jerusalem rebukes you. Is not this a brand plucked out of the fire?'" (Zechariah 3:1-2)

In this instance, the term ha'satan in the original Hebrew is used again to mean the Adversary, but it seems likely that this figure is a representative for the group that was opposing the rebuilding of the Temple, while Joshua represented the righteous returnees. The meaning here is that God is actively on the side of the Jews who wish to reconstruct. His rebuke is against the attempts of that opposing force within the Jewish community to thwart the building of the temple.

The Devil

In a similar vein, the name Lucifer has also been the cause of considerable confusion. Lucifer, a name that only appears one time in the entire Bible, in the book of Isaiah, does not actually refer to Satan or any other spirit, angel, or demon at all.

The oft-quoted verse is actually a condemnation of either one or a dynasty of Babylonian kings— perfectly human at that—who displayed a degree of hubris and arrogance in their time of foreign rule over the Jews that was displeasing to God. The translation of "Lucifer" is "morning star" and the actual denunciation, which is quite extensive, actually begins as follows:

> "How you are fallen from heaven, O Lucifer, son of Dawn!
> How you are cut down to the ground, you who laid the nations
> low! You said in your heart, 'I will ascend to heaven; above the
> stars of God I will set my throne on high; I will sit on the
> mount of assembly in the far north; I will ascend above the
> heights of the clouds, I will make myself like the Most High.'

> But you are brought down to Sheol, to the depths of the Pit.
> Those who see you will stare at you, and ponder over you: 'Is
> this the man who made the earth tremble, who shook king-
> doms, who made the world like a desert and overthrew its cities,
> who did not let his prisoners go home?'" (Isaiah 14:12-17)

The reference to the king of Babylon, and later naming of the subject of the rebuke as "the man who made the earth tremble" makes it fairly clear that Isaiah is indeed speaking of a detested foreign ruler who

Fall of the Rebel Angels *by Giovanni Battista Tiepolo, 1726. The association of Lucifer with the fall of Satan in the familiar role of an angel that tried to revolt against God, may actually be a mistaken reading of a scripture passage.*

had treated the Hebrews poorly while they were under his dominion. But later scholars and Church Fathers, including Origen, St. Augustine, and St. Jerome either mistranslated or misread the passage and came to quite a different conclusion as to what had "fallen from heaven."

Instead of understanding the metaphorical reference to the fortunes of this Babylonian king, the term "Lucifer" or "Morning Star" was taken to be a reference to the fall of Satan, the rebel angel, and the bat‐

tle in heaven as described in the New Testament book of Revelation written hundreds of years later. Cementing the confusion over "Lucifer's" identity, was great English writer John Milton, who cast Lucifer‐as‐Satan as the "hero" of his classic 1667 epic poem *Paradise Lost.*

Throughout the Hebrew Bible, it is God alone who is the bringer of plagues, the great flood withstood only by Noah and his ark, destroyer of cities. Satan is never shown to be an evil entity in any of the older Hebrew scripture. There isn't even a Hell in traditional Jewish faith, for Satan to reign over.

The Jewish underworld is not spoken of much in the Tanakh. Almost all of the dead went to Sheol, or the Pit, which was not charged with particular significance as either a place of punishment or reward. It seems that at least according to the descriptions explicitly given in the Hebrew Bible, death is the end:

Above: The Fall of the Rebel Angels *by Gustave Dore, 1866, illustration from John Milton's* Paradise Lost. *Milton's great epic poem cast Lucifer as its protagonist, thus cementing the association of that name with Satan.*

     The Devil

"As the cloud fades and vanishes, so he who goes down to Sheol does not come up; he returns no more to his house, nor does his place know him any more."
(Job 7:9-10)

Judaism is a religion that concentrates on the here and now, but outside of the Tanakh canon text there was a strong and growing movement in the practical practice of Judaism that did believe in Olam Ha-Ba, or the World to Come. The coming to power of the Pharisees seemed to usher in a stronger certainty in an afterlife. The Pharisees were the Persian-influenced faction— descending from that group of returning exiles who made up the intellectual and priestly class, who had returned under the blessing of the Persian Zoroastrian King Cyrus. Many scholars have come to believe that it is this Zoroastrian influence that changes the tenor of the newly developing Christian faith toward new beliefs and new philosophies, separating it from its Jewish roots.

THE CHRISTIAN BIBLE

If Satan and the lesser demons were in short supply in the Hebrew Bible, they are very much in evidence throughout the Christian scriptures. Both in the twenty-seven books of the New Testament accepted as canon by all Christians and also in the additional eighteen books of the deuterocanonical literature

Above: The Damned in Hell, *Master of Palantes Altar, late fifteenth century. Hell as a place of damnation was not a part of the Hebrew Bible. All the dead traditionally went to Sheol, or The Pit.*

(known as the Apocrypha) that are part of the Catholic canon. Some of them are also accepted by Russian and Greek Orthodox faith as well.

There is still little known about Jesus as a historical figure. Most of the biographical information we have about him comes from the Gospel (the first four books of the New Testament) that recounts Jesus' life and works. It is doubtful that these texts were ever intended to be strictly accurate historical accounts though, but rather theological documents that used the story of the life of Christ as the model around which to present their content.

What is known is that Jesus was a preacher who appeared on the scene during yet another period of unrest and upheaval throughout the Near East. The burgeoning Roman Empire, fresh off its victory in the third Punic War and the defeat of the great city-state of Carthage, took Jerusalem in 65 B.C. and there was an ongoing struggle for control of Judea for generations. The struggle ended rather decisively in favor of the Romans following a revolt in A.D. 70 in which the great temple in Jerusalem was destroyed.

Into this ongoing conflict between the Jews and Romans came Jesus of Nazareth, a popular teacher and preacher, who upset many Jewish leaders with his rather radical reinterpretations of God's message. Jesus's followers believed him to be the Son of God, the Messiah who would return to preside over the Last Judgment. They took up the mantle of spreading his message to any who would listen following the crucifixion sometime around A.D. 30. Although initially persecuted heavily under Roman rule for their beliefs, this religion spurred by Jesus' teachings, known today as Christianity, spread anyway, eventually being adopted by Rome and becoming the most influential and popular religion in the world to date.

Building on the base of the Jewish scripture, the Tanakh, the followers of Jesus added their own accounts of God following the arrival of the figure they believed to be the long prophesied Messiah and God's Son. As we shall see, there are more differences than the addition of this Messiah though, between the Hebrew scripture and the Christian. It is within these new books of faith and scripture that the embodiment of all that is evil, the Devil, is truly born.

The power and influence of Satan and demons in the New Testament seems to grow as more time

Right: The Last Judgment by Hieronymus Bosch (1450-1516). Jesus Christ was welcomed by his followers as the Messiah and Son of God, who would return to preside over the prophesied Last Judgment—a common theme of Apocalyptic literature.

The Devil

passes between the actual death of Jesus and the physical writing of the various New Testament texts. The earliest book of the Gospel to be written was Mark, which is generally dated at approximately A.D. 70. The gospels of Matthew and Luke were likely to have been written some ten to fifteen years after Mark, with the gospel of John coming last, somewhere in the neighborhood of A.D. 90 to 95.

Mark offers a view of Satan more similar in tone to that of the Old Testament use of him. The version of Satan's encounter with Jesus (after Jesus' baptism and identification as the Son of God) as told in the book of Mark reads simply as follows:

"In those days Jesus came from Nazareth of Galilee and was baptized by John in the Jordan. And when he came up out of the water, immediately he saw the heavens opened and the Spirit descending upon him like a dove; and a voice came from heaven, 'Thou art my beloved Son; with thee I am well pleased.' The Spirit immediately drove him out into the wilderness. And he was in the wilderness forty days, tempted by Satan; and he was with the wild beasts; and the angels ministered to him."

(Mark 1:9–13)

The usage of "Satan" here is of the ha'satan meaning that was employed in the story of Job—leaving the impression that perhaps this story is supposed to have a similar meaning. Jesus is tested by Satan to make sure he is ready for the great tasks ahead of him.

Contrast this simple, relatively offhand mention of the encounter in the wilderness in the book of Mark, with the much more elaborate version in Matthew, written perhaps a generation later, that offers quite a different spin on the events:

Above: Satan Tries to Tempt Christ in the Forest. *The story of the temptation of Christ as told in the Gospel of Matthew marks a radical change from Satan's more benign role in the Old Testament.*

The Devil

"Then Jesus was led up by the Spirit into the wilderness to be tempted by the devil. And he fasted forty days and forty nights, and afterward he was hungry. And the tempter came and said to him, 'If you are the Son of God, command these stones to become loaves of bread.' But he answered, 'It is written, "Man shall not live by bread alone, but by every word that proceeds from the mouth of God." '

"Then the devil took him to the holy city, and set him on the pinnacle of the temple, and said to him, 'If you are the Son of God, throw yourself down; for it is written, "He will give his angels charge of you," and "On their hands they will bear you up, lest you strike your foot against a stone." Jesus said to him, 'Again it is written, "You shall not tempt the Lord your God." '

"Again, the devil took him to a very high mountain, and showed him all the kingdoms of the world and the glory of them; and he said to him, 'All these I will give you, if you will fall down and worship me.'

"Then Jesus said to him, 'Begone, Satan! for it is written, "You shall worship the Lord your God and him only shall you serve." ' Then the devil left him, and behold, angels came and ministered to him." (Matthew 4:1-11)

Here we have the beginnings of something else entirely—a Satan who goes beyond his previous role of simply carrying out God's orders. This Satan makes a specific offer of worldly possessions and power in exchange for worship. This is a new wrinkle indeed, Satan offering himself as an alternative to God. It is in this new wrinkle that many scholars see the continuing influence of the Zoroastrian tradition coming in. Remember that the Zoroastrians believed in one god, Ahura Mazda, but also in a supremely evil spirit—Anghra Mainyu—who stands in direct opposition to him.

Also similar to Zoroastrianism, the Christian doctrine developed an apocalyptic vision that was to settle the question of good and evil for all time. The word apocalypse comes from the Greek *apokalypsis* meaning "something uncovered" or "revealed." The common idea in apocalyptic stories, prophecies, or visions is that of a break between the current age and some glorious, and sometimes terrible, future time to come. The stories often feature a great cosmic battle determining the fate of the world and its inhabitants.

The tradition of apocalyptic literature, although having its roots in Zoroastrianism, spread to Judaism in works such as the book of Daniel and the apocryphal book of Enoch. The most famous apocalyptic text though, is the one that was adopted into the canon of the New Testament—the Apocalypse of John—also known as the book of Revelation.

The tone of Revelation (as with most apocalyptic literature) is dark, violent, and terrifying. For the Last Judgment, even Jesus, who throughout so much of the New Testament is portrayed as a gentle teacher, appears here as a fierce warrior, swooping in on a great white horse, sword drawn to smite the wicked. There are earthquakes, meteors hitting the earth, waters being poisoned, and great and horrible word pictures painted of suffering and wrath. It is in Revelation that we get the Biblical reference to the fall of Satan from heaven, and the descriptions of

Above: Hell as seen in the fresco of the Last Judgment *by Giotto (1276-1337). The apocalyptic visions presented in the Book of Revelation contained vivid descriptions of cataclysmic destruction, fire, and death.*

destruction, plague, fire, and sulphurous pits that so heavily influenced the depiction of Hell.

It is believed that the book of Revelation was written in approximately A.D. 90, well in the midst of the struggles against Rome. Modern scholars view many of the seemingly fantastic symbols of the vision to actually represent an allegorical rant against Rome and the heavy persecution faced by early Christian believers under Roman rule. But as scholars have pointed out, the original target of this invective does not limit its power. The symbols used in the prophecy are complex enough, and the history of man repetitive enough, that they can be (and indeed have been) reapplied again and again to suit the needs of various interpreters at different times. It foretold the end of the world many saw coming at the end of the first millennium and, 1000 years later, it foretold the end many saw coming at the end of the second.

The picture of Satan that emerges in all this is one that will be pieced together from various references, some explicit, to give us a decidedly more aggressive and malevolent spirit from anything that appeared in the earlier Hebrew scriptures. In the book of Revelation itself, we get the image from Chapter 12 describing the great battle in heaven with the forces of good led by archangel Michael, where: "that great dragon was cast out, that old serpent, who is called the Devil and Satan, who seduceth the whole

Above: Damned souls burning in fires of Hell, from Polyptych of Last Judgment *by Rogier van der Weyden (1400-64), Flemish. The Last Judgment leaves no room for the wicked, those found to be unworthy of salvation were promised eternal torment.*

Saint Michael after Guido Reni. The only two angels mentioned by name in the Bible are God's messenger Gabriel, and the great Michael, credited in the book of Revelation with defeating Satan and his minions, driving them out of heaven.

world; and he was cast unto the earth, and his angels were thrown down with him." Some scholars have drawn comparisons between this battle and the defeat by the Canaanite god Baal of the great beast Lotan or Leviathan, particularly with the characterization of Satan as a dragon/serpent.

It is the marriage of this Revelation reference, with a couple of descriptions in a different ancient work—the apocryphal book of Enoch—that has filled in and fleshed out the identification of Satan with the fallen angel. Dating from the second century B.C., Enoch, another great apocalyptic work, is filled with stories about God's angels that never got accepted into the mainstream Hebrew scripture. One angel, in particular, Azazel embarks upon a relationship with mankind that leads to sin:

"And Azazel taught men to make swords, and knives, and shields, and breastplates, and made known to them the metals of the earth and the art of working them, and bracelets, and ornaments, and the use of antimony, and the beautifying of the eyelids, and all kinds of costly stones, and all coloring tinctures. And there arose much godlessness, and they committed fornication, and they were led astray, and became corrupt in all their ways." Enoch 8:1-3

Other angels are shown becoming mixed up sinfully with humans, but Azazel is singled out for God's particular wrath:

Right: Satan's Flight Through Chaos, engraving by Gustave Dore, 1866. The angel Azazel, associated strongly with Satan in traditional literature, is ordered to be bound in a barren and rocky place in the Book of Enoch.

     The Devil

"And the whole earth has been corrupted through the works that were taught by Azazel: to him ascribe all sin." (Enoch 10:8-9)

This ascribing of all sin to one particular angel, Azazel, might certainly be seen as having been influenced from the Zoroastrian font of all evil, Anghra Mainyu. The wicked angel Azazel and his cohorts meet a familiar sounding preordained end:

"…and I saw a horrible thing: a great fire there which burnt and blazed, and the place was cleft as far as the abyss, being full of great descending columns of fire: neither its extent or magnitude could I see, nor could I conjecture. Then I said: 'How fearful is the place and how terrible to look upon!' Then Uriel answered me, one of the holy angels who was with me, and said unto me: 'Enoch, why hast thou such fear and affright?' And I answered: 'Because of this fearful place, and because of the spectacle of the pain.' And he said unto me: 'This place is the prison of the angels, and here they will be imprisoned forever.' " (Enoch 22:7-10)

Further cementing the association of Azazel with Satan is this mention in Enoch:

"And again the Lord said to Raphael: 'Bind Azazel hand and foot, and cast him into the darkness: and make an opening in the desert, which is in Dudael, and cast him therein. And place upon him rough and jagged rocks, and cover him with darkness, and let him abide there forever, and cover his face that he may not see light. And on the day of the great judgment he shall be cast into the fire.' " (Enoch 10:4-7)

Above: Angel Locking the Devil into Hell, from the Apocalypse engravings by Albrecht Dürer, 1498. Many references in various apocalyptic texts portend similar visions that mark the end of time.

This rather closely mirrors the following verses from a chapter of Revelation:

> "Then I saw an angel coming down from heaven with the key of the abyss and a great chain in his hands. He seized the dragon, that serpent of old, the Devil or Satan, and chained him up for a thousand years, he threw him into the abyss, shutting and sealing it over him, so that he might seduce the nations no more till the thousand years were over. After that he must be let loose for a short while." (Revelation 20:1-3)

It is the similarities in these two apocalyptic texts, Enoch and Revelation that combine to create what became the popular vision of Satan as the fallen angel, the seducer, and tempter of mankind. As we shall see, in their efforts at understanding and consolidating the various tenets of their faith, early Christian scholars and Church founders combed through the books of the various scriptures, seeking out any references to dragons, serpents, and beasts, and associating them with Satan and his underlings.

One well-known image of evil, often associated with the Devil and his works that is not mentioned in the book of Revelation, is the Antichrist. The term "antichrist" only appears five times in the New Testament, all in the two books that comprise the Epistles of John. All five usages are similar to this one:

> "Who is the liar? It is the man who denies that Jesus is the Christ. Such a man is the antichrist—he denies the Father and the Son." (1 John 2:22)

Antichrist, here and in the other nearly identical verses that use the term, simply means any person who does not accept that Jesus is the Son of God. How then, did Antichrist become so closely associated with interpretation of the apocalyptic vision of Revelation? Some scholars believe it may be a simple confusion of three different men named John—one the writer of the Gospel of John and the first book of John, the second man named John who is credited with the books 2 John and 3 John, and lastly the third man named John who wrote Revelation. Thinking that all these texts were written by the same person, early Christian scholars sought to make connections between them, perhaps associating Antichrist with the "beast" in Revelation, the one with that most famous numerical mark:

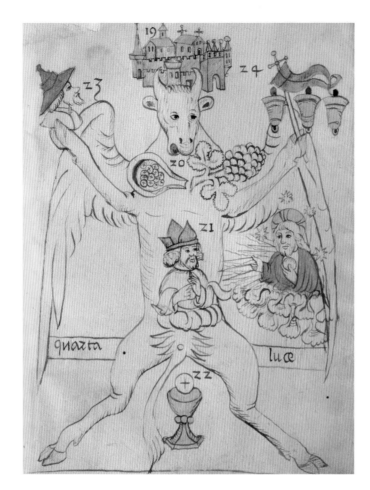

"…and by the signs which it is allowed to work in the presence of the beast, it deceives those who dwell on earth, bidding them make an image for the beast which was wounded by the sword and yet lived; and it was allowed to give breath to the image of the beast so that the image of the beast should even speak, and to cause those who would not worship the image of the beast to be slain. It causes all, both small and great, both rich and poor, both free and slave, to be marked on the right hand or the forehead, so that no one can buy or sell unless he has the mark, that is, the name of the beast or the number of its name. This calls for wisdom: let him who has understanding reckon the number of the beast, for it is a human number, its number is 666." (Revelation 13:14-18)

The beast, like Antichrist, is portrayed as a deceiver. Scholars point to one further prophecy of a liar, from the New Testament book 2 Thessalonians. The prophecy calls for the coming of a "lawless one," and his coming is considered one of the signs that the return of Jesus is nigh. Like the beast, this "lawless

Above: Antichrist illustration from a fourteenth-century Latin manuscript. The Antichrist, here pictured as a bull, often gets associated with the "beast" in Revelation, even though there is no mention of Antichrist in that apocalyptic book.

The Devil

one" gains an association with Satan and comes to be viewed and depicted as Satan's henchman. The popular conception of Antichrist then, like Lucifer, is a reference and association made after the fact—a series of connections drawn from disparate sources that combine to create a much more richly fleshed out history and explanation of these often mysterious symbols.

The adoption and spread of Christianity in the next centuries would see an unprecedented rush to further elaborate and connect the stories and symbols found in the scriptures. This next period in the Devil's history would see him gain his most familiar shape and position.

The defeat of the Antichrist, panel from La Leyenda de San Miguel *by Master of Arguis, c. 1450, Spain.*
The Antichrist as a particular entity or character, is generally considered to be a creation of Christian scholars
looking for connections in the scriptures.

CHAPTER THREE:

The Devil Grows Horns (and Teeth)

Certain doctrines of Christianity—including a theoretical equality of all men before God, a promise of forgiveness for repented sins, and a message of hope for redemption—made it an attractive system of belief for the poor and humble masses. But early Christians faced a tough road in their quest to spread and practice their chosen faith in peace. The religion was spread from its initial center of Judea at first by the original apostles and most aggressively by Paul of Tarsus. Paul concentrated his efforts on spreading the word of Jesus to Gentiles (non-Jews) and was so successful at his conversion efforts that, by the time of his death, he had established Christian churches throughout the eastern Mediterranean. Paul, like the original apostle Peter and many others, was executed by the Romans on charges of stirring up civil unrest. The word continued to grow and spread in spite of intermittent persecution, however, and the issuance of the Edict of Milan by Emperor Constantine in A.D. 313 put an end to any persecution by decreeing an official tolerance for all religions within the Roman Empire. Constantine was the first Roman Emperor sympathetic to Christianity.

Free to grow unhindered now, Christianity continued to spread, but there was still no real organized Church at this point. Different groups in different cities and regions held differing views of what the Christian faith should be. Texts and accounts that were considered authoritative in some sectors were thought to be heretical and dangerous in others. Growing up in this period of scattered ideas and theories came the Christian Gnostics. They focused on the gaining of spiritual knowledge as the key to salvation and tended to downplay the divinity of Jesus, viewing him more in the role of teacher and revealer of hidden truths. This Gnostic movement peaked in the second century and had been almost completely stamped out by the fifth.

Right: Archangel Michael defeats devils, from St. Michael altarpiece c. 1240. The spread of Christianity picked up speed in the centuries following the death of Jesus Christ.

Most scholars date the real organization of the Church as a unified entity to the holding of the Council of Nicea in A.D. 325, which sought to identify and sort out common beliefs from among all these varying local customs, thus offering some unity to this burgeoning religious movement. It was at this Council of Nicea meeting that the official divinity of Jesus was established and codified as Christian doctrine. In A.D. 330 Constantine built the city of Constantinople to be the new capital, and Christianity was eventually made the official state religion of the Roman Empire.

THE EARLY CHURCH FATHERS

We have seen how the idea of Satan grew and changed from his relatively benign appearances in the Hebrew bible, to the more aggressive tempter and deceiver of the newer Christian scriptures. But what influence did these early Church Fathers have on the view of Satan?

In what became known as the Alexandrian school of thought, allegorical interpretation of the Bible was promoted, the divinity of Jesus was considered paramount, and the human and divine aspects of Christ's nature were thought to be tightly interwoven. The early Christian Fathers, translators,

Above: Saint Jerome in Penitence in the Wilderness *by Luigi Asiolo (1817–77), Italian. Saint Jerome was one of the most influential of the early Church Fathers, a translator, interpreter, and scholar.*

interpreters, and scholars such as Clement, Origen, Augustine, and Jerome were instrumental in the subtle, and sometimes not so subtle, recasting of scriptural references to suit their views throughout the fourth century. Origen, Clement's successor, was one of the most influential of the early Fathers in establishing allegorical connections and seeking deeper meanings within the actual text of the biblical books. Augustine also built on Origen's interpretive view of scripture, offering that the Bible had to be read not only literally, but also allegorically and morally for the true and deeper meaning to come to light.

It is this habit of recasting and interpreting that led to such associations as St. Jerome's fourth century A.D. translation and understanding of the description of Lucifer, the "Morning Star" in the book of Isaiah, as a reference to the fallen Satan as described in Revelation. Further connections were drawn between the serpent/dragon description of Satan in Revelation and any mention of serpents in the entire Bible, up to and including the serpent in the Garden of Eden. It never seemed to be an issue of any concern to the Fathers that they were working backwards through the scriptures—taking the most modern references and using them as the basis for conclusions they were drawing about the most ancient. The fact that at least one of the great original Church Fathers, Origen, was later condemned as a heretic shows how transitory belief in some of these views could be.

CONVERTING THE PAGANS

For the newly official state religion, what to do with the non-Christian local inhabitants of various parts of the far-flung empire became an important question. There are reports that after being designated the official religion of the Roman Empire, the formerly persecuted Christians were often the ones leaning hard on local populations to convert in great numbers. Under the Emperor Theodosian, a series of decrees were issued in the fourth century A.D., which rescinded much of the religious toleration and freedoms that had been granted by Constantine in the Edict of Milan only some thirty years prior.

The Theodosian decrees marked the end of this period of official toleration and Christianity and Judaism were the only two religions allowed within the territories held by the Empire. Pagan and Gnostic believers suffered under this new policy, with old pagan temples being either converted to Christian use

or destroyed and many priests and priestesses were persecuted and exiled. In the first of what was to become a long and ugly line of events to come, Bishop Priscillian in Spain, a teacher of some Gnostic ideas, became the first heretic executed by fellow Christians for religious reasons.

Even potentially catastrophic events could not seem to stop the wildfire spread of Christianity. In A.D. 451, following decades of the type of political infighting and power struggles that would come to mark much of the Church's history, the faith finally split in two, with the Western half of the faith being controlled by the Pope in Rome, and the Eastern part by the Bishops in Byzantium. This separation eventually resulted in two different Churches, made formal in A.D. 1054—the Roman Catholic in the West and the Greek Orthodox in the East. The second major event to rock the potential power and stability of the Church was the attacking and invasion of Rome by the Goths and other Germanic tribes throughout the fifth century which destroyed much of the Roman Empire. Such was the power of the appeal of Christianity though, that rather than bringing their religious faith to their newly conquered territory, the Church instead managed to convert the invaders.

The general, and mostly successful, policy of the advancing Christian faith became one of absorption and assimilation. The idea was to adopt whatever aspects of the already existing local religions were deemed harmless enough that they didn't pose a threat to the vital tenets of the Church doctrine and these would be kept to ease along the conversion of the inhabitants into Christianity. For the most part, the effort to absorb and assimilate the pagan religions was successful, with one notable exception.

The ancient fertility cult religions—perhaps as old as humankind itself and entrenched in various parts of Europe and the Mediterranean—seemed to have an unbreakably strong hold on their followers.

Above: Relief sculpture, Austria. Believers in the old pagan gods came in for serious persecution once Christianity was declared the official state religion of the Roman Empire.

The Devil

When faced with the power of this ancient tradition, the practice of absorbing and accepting aspects of the local faith was insufficient for the task. The tried and true process of demonizing these beliefs was used to do the job instead.

SATAN GROWS HORNS

Anthropologists tell us that the Horned God may well be the oldest deity recognized by humankind. Appearances on cave paintings dating back as far as 10,000 B.C. place evidence of, at least, the precursor to the Horned God well before the earliest known civilization in Sumer or Jericho. One such painting found in the Caverne des Trois Frères at Ariège, France, depicts a male figure who seems to be affecting some sort of dance or prance, while wearing a pair of antlers on his head. Totemic god cults continue to appear, in one form or another, down through the centuries in many cultures, with particular concentration in Europe and the Mediterranean.

There were various incarnations these horned deities took. Pan Pangenetor in Greek mythology was built on the satyr model, half goat and half man, and was only one of the horned gods in common worship. Another popular and powerful version was the cult of Dionysus, honored all over the Mediterranean basin. Almost always, as was the case with Pan and Dionysus, the Horned God has a strong association with fertility, prosperity, and also with death. The totemic aspect of worshipping these deities usually involved the

Above: Detail of Satan from The Last Judgment *by Jacopo da Bologna c. 1350. The near-total association of Satan with traits of the ancient pagan Horned God represents one of the most thorough examples of demonizing in history.*

belief that the spirit of the animal could be absorbed through proper ritual, and so dancing, chanting, sacrifice, and affecting the appearance of a horned animal were common worship practices.

So what was the Devil supposed to look like before he began to take on attributes drawn at least partially from satyr or Horned God figures? Biblical descriptions of Satan, in the book of Revelation at least, draw comparisons with dragons and serpents. But there was a period when the various interpretations of Church Fathers had not yet settled on just what sort of beings Satan and his minions were. According to Cassian, and agreed to by Origen:

"When we proclaim that there are spiritual natures such as angels we must not think that they are incorporeal. They have a body which makes them subsist; but this body is much more subtle than ours."

This somewhat vague view was accepted by the Church for centuries, until replaced by the dictum of Honoré of Autun, which came to the slightly more precise and differentiated conclusion that:

"Angels have ethereal bodies, the demons have aerial bodies, men have terrestrial bodies."

At some point, it also seems to have been agreed that demons could at least assume material bodies some of the time. By around A.D. 1000, representations of demons, and particularly of Satan, began to take on the appearance of a grotesque combination of fearsome features. One possibility as to the sudden

Above: Devil in a stooping position. The attributes of totemic pagan deities such as Dionysus, who was often associated with a stag or a goat, worked their way into depictions of demons and the Devil.

appearance of these representations is that they coincide with the holding of the Council of Cluny in A.D. 956. It was decided here, that stricter religious rule enforcement was needed and that the Church needed to do a better job of stamping out heretical practices and ideas.

The choice of goat as a base animal for depictions of the Devil may have additional roots beyond the connection with the popular, sensual god Pan (or Dionysus who also got associated with the goat on occasion). There is a passage in the book of Matthew that describes what the scenario surrounding the Last Judgment is going to be like:

> "When the Son of man comes in his glory, and all the angels with him, then he will sit on his glorious throne. Before him will be gathered all the nations, and he will separate them one from another as a shepherd separates the sheep from the goats, and he will place the sheep at his right hand, but the goats at the left." (25:31-33)

So here we have a biblical reference to goats representing the not-chosen, the unrighteous. This consideration, along with the pressure the Church must have been feeling on some level to strike out at the veneration of traditional pagan gods like Pan, led to not merely the demonizing of these Horned God figures, but the transformation of them into the very embodiment of the most fearsome and evil symbol in the Christian canon.

This is not to suggest that the demonizing of the Horned God was a deliberate or planned action on the part of any particular individual. It is unlikely that there was a secret committee drawn up for the sole purpose of establishing rules for the depiction of Satan as a satyrlike

Right: Notre Dame de Paris Cathedral gargoyle. Attempts were often made to incorporate elements of the local religions where it could be done so harmlessly. Whether gargoyles represent incorporation or demonizing remains unclear.

creature. The process was almost certainly a gradual one, a developing language of art that evolved to communicate and illustrate ideas that were in the popular imagination.

THE MEDIEVAL MIND

When considering the evolution of faith and the religious ideas and methods during this period that appear barbaric and cruel to the modern sensibility, it is important to keep the medieval worldview in mind. The spread and ministering of the faith was conducted, for the most part, by local parish priests who had little formal training. Books were expensive, laborious to copy, and rare.

The tales of demons and other supernatural events taught by their local priests probably didn't seem farfetched to the local populace at all. Disease and death were much closer neighbors to men and women in medieval times than they are to us now. Life expectancy before 1500 or so is estimated to have been in the neighborhood of 30 years. Otherwise young, strong people died routinely from diseases and accidents that would be easily treated today. Childbirth was a genuinely risky proposition for women and it has been estimated that the infant mortality rate in the first year of life may have approached 30 percent. There was no understanding of sanitation or the ways disease was spread, no modern medicine or drug therapy, and often the "treatments" offered the ill, such as bloodletting, made health worse instead of better.

In this narrow world, the power and influence of the Church was incomparable to anything we can imagine today. Medieval people were extremely concerned with understanding religion and following the rules correctly. Their souls were at stake, after all. Daily life was difficult and precarious enough without fear of eternal damnation and the hope of entering the Kingdom of Heaven provided many with desperately needed solace.

Above: The Expulsion of Lucifer, *fourteenth-century English psalter. The satyr/Horned God model remained the most enduring depiction of the Devil and demons for centuries.*

In this desire for knowledge and under-standing, medieval Christian clergy, scholars, and artists expended much time and effort in attempting to map out and codify as many aspects of their faith as possible. One result was the development of the list known to us still as the Seven Deadly Sins. The first such list was believed to have been created by a monk named Evagrius of Pontus and his list actually con-tained eight items, in order of severity: gluttony, lust, avarice, sadness, anger, acedia, vainglory, and pride. Acedia is a Greek-rooted term and means indifference or uncaring. The severity scale in Evagrius's system is based upon increas-ing levels of concern with the self, landing pride in the top spot.

This list was amended by Pope Gregory in the sixth century, who cut the list length to seven and changed some of the terms. Gregory's list went (again in order of severity): lust, gluttony, avarice, sadness, anger, envy, pride. Gregory combined the sins of vainglory and pride into one and, likewise, rolled acedia into sadness. He also added envy.

Pride still tops the list here, but according to Gregory, for a different reason than Evagruis. Gregory's

Above: Leprous Job in bed, fifteenth-century manuscript Bible, said to belong to Pope John XXII. The process of making books in the Middle Ages was laborious and time consuming, and would remain so until the com-ing of the printing press in the late 15th century.

severity scale is based upon how greatly the various sins "offended against love." Later theologians, most notably Saint Thomas Aquinas, disputed the idea that the seriousness or severity of the sins should, or even could, be ranked in this way. Also later, some time in the 17th century, the sin of sadness was replaced with sloth.

As depicted in Ernst and Johanna Lehner's *Picture Book of Devils, Demons and Witchcraft*, each of the Seven Deadly Sins was matched up with specific punishments in Hell:

Sin	Punishment
Pride	broken on the wheel
Envy	put in freezing water
Anger	dismemberment
Sloth	thrown in snake pit
Greed	boiled in cauldrons of oil
Gluttony	force-fed rats, toads, and snakes
Lust	smothered in fire and brimstone

The Church thought it to be very important to teach all lay people the Deadly Sins, as well as the corresponding Heavenly Virtues: faith, hope, charity, fortitude, justice, temperance, and prudence. It was hoped that having an understanding of both sets of behaviors would help people to understand the rewards or potential consequences of their choices.

The wages of sin were fully illustrated in many works of art displayed in churches. Such painting, sculpture, and stained glass were important teaching tools in a time when illiteracy was near universal. Depictions of Hell were a quick and visceral reminder that there is more to worry about than the here and now.

One of the most common configurations for Hell was a stratified system—much like the original conception of the Seven Deadly Sins, the worse the offense, the deeper into Hell the placement. The most

Left: Hell, from table-top with the Seven Deadly Sins *by Hieronymus Bosch. Each of the Deadly Sins was reported to have a corresponding punishment in Hell.*

famous, and influential tiered system of Hell is certainly the one derived by Dante Alighieri in the Inferno (A.D. 1314) book of his *Divina Commedia*.

The central conceit of *Divina Commedia*, is that the great poet Virgil (writer of the *Aeneid*) acts as a guide to Dante on his journey through Paradiso (Heaven), Purgatorio (Purgatory), and Inferno (Hell). The vision of Hell we are given is an arrangement of nine circles (perfectly counterbalanced by the nine circles of Heaven) arranged so that lesser sins leave one closer to the earth's surface, while worsening transgression pushes a damned soul deeper into the bowels of the earth.

The notion that Hell was literally located underground was a very common one and seemed to be supported by scriptural references dating back to the Old Testament. The Hebrew underworld Sheol was also known as the Pit:

> "I will make the nations quake at the sound of its fall, when I cast it down to Sheol with
> those who go down to the Pit; and all the trees of Eden, the choice and best of Lebanon,
> all that drink water, will be comforted in the nether world." (Ezekiel 31:16)

Dante's system is a complex elaboration, arranging the circles of Hell, with the first level being Limbo—reserved for the unbaptised and pagans who were otherwise virtuous. Dante's host, Virgil, a pre-Christian Roman is a denizen of Limbo.

Winding downwards, the second level contains the lustful, the third gluttons, the fourth the covetous, and the fifth the ever-rioting angry. In the fifth circle of Hell are the River Styx and the City of Dis, in which all of Lower Hell is located. Being consigned to Lower Hell, in Dante's estimation, requires sins that are deliberate acts against God (versus the sins that land one in Upper Hell, mere weakness of will and character by comparison). The sixth level of Hell features heretics. Below them in level seven are those who have been "violent against nature and self" (homosexuals and suicides). Level eight was for perpetrators of fraud, and lastly, the very bottom of Hell, the frozen lake Cocytus is where we find Satan himself. Dante's vision of Satan is a three-headed beast with:

Right: Last Judgment *(detail) by Fra Angelico, fifteenth century. It was widely believed that Hell was located below the Earth's surface and the idea of a tiered arrangement was popular after Dante's Inferno.*

     The Devil

Dante and Virgil with damned in Hell from the Divine Comedy, 14th century. The great pre-Christian Roman poet Virgil occupied Limbo, the first tier of Hell reserved for the unbaptized.

"Two mighty wings, enormous as became A bird so vast. Sails never such I saw Outstretch'd on the wide sea. No plumes had they, But were in texture like a bat, and these He flapp'd i' th' air, that from him issued still."
(Canto XXXIV)

Dante's three heads of Satan were each busy gnashing at the three worst traitors Dante could think of: Judas, betrayer of Jesus Christ, and Brutus and Cassius, betrayers of Julius Caesar. It would be interesting to speculate as to whether Dante would decide to replace any of those figures were he alive today.

Dante's vision of a three-headed Satan didn't ever become as common in the artistic depictions we see of him (although that configuration certainly did get represented), as the satyr/Horned God model. However the description of batlike wings was an extremely popular choice.

Adding to the already difficult task of virtuous daily living, there were always the dangers of tempta-tion one had to vigilantly be on the lookout for. The notion of Satan or his minions as an active, aggressive suitor for the baser desires of humankind is an idea that we saw in the Gospel of Matthew's

Right: Fall of the Rebel Angels *by Guillermo Talarn, fifteenth century. Dante's description of Satan having wings like a bat was a common depiction. Here Satan's falling minions comprise a number of demonic types.*

version of the temptation of Jesus in the wilderness. From that passage, Satan offers Jesus "all the kingdoms of the world and the glory of them" (Matthew 4) in exchange for worship, and Church scholars came to the conclusion that the Devil must actually have dominion over the earth to be empowered to make such an offer.

Prince of this World becomes another of Satan's many names, and study and depiction of figures such as Saint Anthony of Egypt became popular entrees into the discussion of temptation and how to deal with it.

Saint Anthony is best known as the founder of the Christian monastic movement and was born in the mid-third century A.D. to wealthy parents. One day, following a gospel message linking piety and poverty, Anthony gave away all his worldly goods and set out to imitate the life of the Apostles. Saint Anthony's best-known writing deals with the duties of a spiritual existence. One of the central struggles of this spiritual life, for Saint Anthony at least, seemed to be constant battle against the demons of temptation. The biography of Anthony, written between A.D. 356 and 362 by his contemporary, Athanasius, contains some startling and physical images. Here, when Satan's initial campaign of whispered temptation fails:

> "…he attacked the young man, disturbing him by night and harassing him by day, so that even the onlookers saw the struggle which was going on between them. The one would suggest foul thoughts and the other counter them with prayers: the one fire him with lust the other, as one who seemed to blush, fortify his body with faith, prayers, and fasting. And the devil, unhappy

Above: Saint Dunston pulls the nose of the Devil. Legend reports that eleventh-century Saint Dunston grabbed Satan's nose with hot tongs in order to enjoin further attempts at temptation.

The Devil

wight, one night even took upon him the shape of a woman and imitated all her acts simply to beguile Antony. But he, his mind filled with Christ and the nobility inspired by Him, and considering the spirituality of the soul, quenched the coal of the other's deceit."

The painting by Flemish painter Hieronymus Bosch—quite possibly the most famous portrayer of sin in western art—depicts some of the many struggles reported by Anthony in his biography. The solution to all this temptation, Anthony concludes, is a steady occupation with manual labor.

All of these ideas about the human struggle to lead a virtuous life in the face of hardship and temptation were central to existence in the Middle Ages. God and Satan both were very real in the medieval mind, and locked in a constant battle for men's eternal souls. The strength and passion of these beliefs provided doubtless comfort and solace to many of the faithful. But, as we shall see, the unwavering certitude of some of these attitudes also had some darker implications for anyone running afoul of God's plan.

Above: The Temptation of Saint Anthony *by Hieronymus Bosch. Saint Anthony of Egypt's biography included numerous reports of very aggressive temptations by the Devil. Anthony was a popular subject for painters to illustrate the strength of virtue.*

CHAPTER FOUR:

The Devil Takes Center Stage—Burnings and Bargains

THE INQUISTION

After the Church had consolidated its position of authority in the early Middle Ages, it began to act to conserve and maintain this power. Crucial to maintaining order, it was thought, was dealing with and eliminating heretic groups before they took hold and became a serious threat.

Following the stamping out of the Gnostic sects, which was largely accomplished by the fifth century, the Church didn't really have to deal with large-scale heretic groups until the advent of the Catharist movement. This sprang up in France in the eleventh century and began to spread, at a rate alarming to the Church. The Catharists' (and later Waldensians') popularity was in part due to disillusionment with the Church, which many found, by the eleventh and twelfth centuries, to be systemically corrupt. In many quarters, the Waldensians are considered the true forerunners of the Protestant Reformation.

The Church had become the most powerful institution in Europe, with great wealth and influence, and the Pope's power was equal to if not surpassing any head of state. The ostensibly celibate clergy often had well-known illegitimate children and the sale of indulgences to fund the construction of the great cathedrals often put the favor of the Church up for grabs to any who could pay the price.

The establishment of the first stage of the Inquisition, charged with actively seeking out and dealing with heresy, came at the order of Pope Innocent III in 1216. Dominic de Guzman (founder of the Dominican order) was asked to train a group of ecclesiastical representatives to police and eradicate heretical activity. The scale and scope of the investigations was widened by Pope Gregory IX and, by

Right: The Ship of Fools *(detail) by Hieronymus Bosch. Widespread corruption within the Catholic Church became the subject of increasing public notice and dissatisfaction, paving the way for the Protestant Reformation.*

1255, the Inquisition was in full swing in Central and Western Europe.

The early stages of the Inquisition focused almost entirely on the stamping out of the bourgeoning heresy threat posed by the Catharists and Waldensians, and witchcraft was of minor importance. That was to change drastically however, in later centuries with witches taking the brunt of the frenzy. Whereas the heretics were charged with changing or reject- ing certain aspects of Church doctrine, the main accusations leveled at witches were the much more actively malevolent crimes of worship of and consort with the Devil.

THE PROTESTANT REFORMATION

The witch-hunting craze, which lasted from c. 1450–1792, was at least in part a reaction to the massive social upheavals churning through Europe. The stranglehold influence of the Church on the popular mind and culture of Western society slowly began to lose its uncontested grip under the relentless force of many pressures. The Renaissance, or "rebirth" began in Italy and spread throughout Europe in the 15th and 16th centuries. Believing their civilization to have finally moved past the ignorance and barbarism of the Middle Ages, Renaissance scholars and artists turned back to the Classical empires of ancient Greece and Rome for their inspiration, hoping to usher in a new age of intellectual and artistic growth and achievement.

By mid-15th century, the printing press had changed forever the way in which knowledge and ideas

The Condemned Brought to the Inquisition by Eugenio Lucas (1824–1870). With the accused often considered guilty before the trial even began, the Inquisition became a terrifying weapon of social control.

Left: Auto da fe presided over by Saint Dominic (1170-1221), founder of the Dominican order by Pedro Berruguete. The Inquisition symbolizes for many people the very worst extremes of religious intolerance.

ÆTHERNA IPSE SVAE MENTIS SIMVLACHRA LVTHERVS
EXPRIMIT AT VVLTVS CERA LVCAE OCCIDVOS
M · D · X · X

6. Bildnis Luthers von 1520. Kupferstich der Cranach-Werkstatt

could be spread, and books began to circulate more quickly and more cheaply. Increased trade and capitalism were challenging feudalism as the dominant economic model. In many cases, support for religious reform went hand in hand with desire for other changes to the old establishment.

After the Renaissance, the second major movement to rock the old world order was the Protestant Reformation, begun in 1517 by Martin Luther, which had taken successful hold in many parts of Europe by the close of the century. Luther articulated dissatisfactions with the all but officially institutionalized corruption in the Catholic Church, that were ready to be heard and embraced by a wide audience. Luckily for Luther, the Inquisition had not been established in Germany at the time he attached his 95 Theses to the door of the church in Wittenberg. As it was, Luther was excommunicated for his teachings—had he been in southern France, he would have likely gone to the stake as a heretic.

The relative weakness of the Catholic Church in Germany allowed Protestantism to spread and take hold so thoroughly that when the Church attempted to counter, it was too late to defeat the Protestant movement. The Church

Above: German-born Martin Luther (1483-1546) set the Protestant Reformation in motion in 1517 with his famous nailing of the 95 Theses to the door of the church in Wittenberg

did institute a Counter-Reformation movement, which was a two-pronged attack consisting of an attempt to address the worst abuses within the Church, while simultaneously trying to win back members who had fled to the new Protestant movement—often attempting to affect that persuasion by force.

This period of history, marked on the one hand by the achievement of great artists and thinkers such as Michelangelo and Leonardo da Vinci, was also host to some of the darkest treatment humans have ever visited upon one another. In the name of stamping out heresy and combating the influence of Satan, both the Catholic and Protestant churches would falsely accuse, torture, and murder thousands of people.

THE BURNING TIMES

> "He must not be too quick to subject a witch to examination, but must pay attention to certain signs which will follow. And he must not be too quick for this reason: unless God, through a holy Angel, compels the devil to withold his help from the witch, she will be so insensible to the pains of torture that she will sooner be torn limb from limb than confess any of the truth." (*Malleus Maleficarum*, Part 3, Question XIII)

The word maleficum, which technically translates to mean any kind of crime or wrongdoing, was used to refer to malevolent magic. In the view of Christianity in the Middle Ages, all magic was malevolent by definition under the reasoning that magic only works by an appeal to supernatural powers. God and the

Above: Witches setting town on fire, from Compendium Malleficarum *by Francesco Guazzo, 1626. The casting of spells that could influence matter was a charge frequently leveled against witches.*

angels would certainly never be compelled by a human summons, therefore the only forces who were available to be called upon were demonic. Since no magic could be accomplished without the aid of demons, anyone who engaged in witch-craft (or whatever was determined to fall under the increasingly broad category that got called witchcraft) was making a de facto pact with the Devil.

There was a definite increase in witch prosecutions following the publication of the infamous *Malleus Maleficarum*, or "Witches Hammer" written by Jakob Sprenger and Heinrich Institor Kremer in 1484. The *Malleus Maleficarum* was the first of several published witch-hunting manuals and remained a popular choice for 300 years. Among the contents are methods for identification and capture of witches, and the best ways to use torture to elicit a satisfactory confession.

The Devil absconding on horseback with a witch. The Wild Ride was a common element in descriptions of witchcraft activity. Riding on broomsticks became another popular mode of witch transportation.

The *Malleus Maleficarum* described witchcraft as the worst possible heresy—direct treason against God—and recommended the severest allowable punishment and most thorough methods to deal with it. The essential parts of witchcraft in Sprenger and Kremer's estimation are: the denial of Christian faith, the sacrifice of unbaptized children to Satan, a personal devotion to evil, and sexual congress with the Devil. The reports of witch activity in books such as the *Malleus Maleficarum* and what came out in tri-als, often led to a self-fulfilling cycle of "proof" for these behaviors.

The conductors of the tribunal would torture the accused to obtain a confession for the specific activi-ties that witch-hunting manuals, such as the *Malleus Maleficarum*, told them they ought to be looking for. The more people were convicted and publicly punished or executed for these offenses, the more word

Left: Witches Sabbath *by Frans Francken (1581–1642), Flemish. The details of witches' secret ritual prac-tices often became the subject of intense fascination for the accusers.*

spread about the nature of the purported witchcraft rituals. After a certain point, the accused knew what sorts of activities they would be expected to confess their participation in, and it is believed that in the attempt to appease their prosecutors and perhaps win themselves some mercy, many of the accused would elaborate ever wilder "confessions," which would then be held up as proof of the spreading scourge of witchcraft invading the land. The fact that most people who went on trial were tortured until they gave up the names of their friends and neighbors as their coconspirators surely added to the sudden "epidemic" number of witches who were being rooted out.

The confessions contained vividly detailed accounts of secret meetings that were said to be held at night. These meetings came to be known as sabbats. Sabbats were assemblies of witches and sorcerers in which feasting and ritual dancing laid the groundwork for blasphemous rites, which usually involved desecration of Christian symbols such as crosses which were inverted, stamped, and spat upon. The Inquisitor at a trial in Lyon, France, alleged that the witches in that city were going to Church and receiving communion, only to secret away the host, saving it for later use in maleficium. Another witch was accused of urinating into the holy water font of her local church. These perversions of Church sacraments or desecration of symbols were said to be a demonstration of the witches' utter rejection of and contempt for Christianity, and embrace and active worship of Satan.

Above: Satan forces the Adepts or Alchemists to step on the cross, from Compendium Malleficarum *by Francesco Guazzo, 1626. Accusations of rituals that included the blasphemous use of Christian symbols intensified the emotion involved in witch trials.*

Ritual killing of children (frequently specified as unbaptized children) was another common accusation. Child torture and murder charges certainly added to the emotional intensity of the proceedings, a technique that harkens back to the ancient Hebrew accusations against the worshipers of the foreign god Molech who were said to sacrifice their own children to satisfy the blood lust of that demon god. The witches' murder of children was said to be used for three

purposes: as a simple sacrifice to Satan, for cannibalism among themselves in their ritual feasts, or for mixing into salves or ointments to be used later in black magic spells. The blood of babies was said to be particularly useful in the manufacture of a special salve, which when rubbed on the hands and a stick or broom, could send a witch airborne. Witnesses began to report seeing witches engaged in night rides, either alone astride a broomstick or on the back of some kind of beast in company with Satan.

While the cannibalism charge was usually restricted to the consumption of children (who were reported to be roasted—a method of preparation familiar to anyone who knows of the evil witch from the fairy tale Hansel and Gretel) there were also occasionally allegations made that witches dug up corpses for the purpose of eating them at their feasts.

Another standard activity at witch sabbats was conjuring or invoking the Devil to appear so that those present could offer him worship. When the Devil did appear, the witches took part in

Above: Children admitted to the Sabbath, from Compendium Malleficarum *by Francesco Guazzo, 1626. Charges, which included abuse or endangerment of children, were also used to build public support for the harshest possible crackdown on witches.*

three ceremonies to honor him. The first was sacrifice—either one of those aforementioned mur-dered children, or else animals, money, even a part of the witch's own body were used. The second type of ceremony was homage, usually some sort of sworn oath, followed by the third ceremony, the obscene kiss. The obscene kiss, or *osculum infame*, was sometimes performed on the Devil's hand or foot, but most often was offered to the Devil's buttocks or genitals. In a show of appreciation to his followers, the Devil then was reported to sign his faithful with a mark of some sort. The exact size, shape, and placement of this mark was always variable and vague enough that most accused witch-es, after being stripped and shorn head to toe could have one found upon them somewhere in the form of an unfortunate mole or freckle.

The most sensational and luridly described facet of witch activity, of course, was the sex orgy. These were both performed with Satan, and simply among the witches themselves. Ritual copulation with Satan was said to be unpleasant and frightening for the participants, done out of fear and loyalty, not for pleasure. The Devil's body is described in the now traditional satyr type with horns. He is hairy, with bony limbs and hooked, taloned, or cloven feet. Many accounts go so far as to describe his sex organ as being cold and soft. The lengths to which some of the Inquisitorial authors go into details of the sexual orgies, including sodomy, homosexuality, and bestiality do seem to strike many historians today as saying much more about the frustrated and prurient interests of the writers than anything that went on with the accused.

When we look at the crimes and heresies that witches are alleged to have committed in their trials, it is nearly impossible to not be reminded of the traditional pagan fertility religious rituals—certainly still being carried out in many parts of Europe—as the model for a good number of the accuser's fantasies.

Many of the feasts, dances, and conjuring descriptions can be seen to have been adapted from the ancient worship dances. The manufacture and use of magical salves and powders certainly has reference to the folk medicines and herbal preparations many local wise women and midwives had knowledge of.

Left: Devil Appearing. This woodcut shows a witch using ritual to conjure the Devil. Note the presence of a broom in her hand.

Overleaf: The Witches Sabbath by Goya. A common worship ritual for traditional pagan fertility cult groups included dances in which one member of the group dressed to affect the image of the Horned God.

Above: Sixteenth-century woodcut depicting a witch riding a goat to meet the Devil. Over time, the more common elements of witchcraft charges, such as night rides, became nearly standard.

Right: Woodcut of witches standing at cauldron from alchemy book by Ulrich Molitor, 1487. Women who functioned as healers frequently found their efforts turned against them as accusations of witchcraft.

The reports of night rides correspond to another ancient mythic tradition of the Wild Hunt or Wild Ride in which the souls of deceased warriors were said to go on a destructive nocturnal rampage, and in some traditions, this Wild Hunt was led by the female goddess of both fertility and killing—Artemis/Hecate.

Doubtless, some of the women (and the phenomenon was directed toward women in the vast majority of cases) accused of witchcraft did practice some type of magic and believe in some of these ancient folk traditions. Many were older wise-women or healers. But it is doubtful that many, if any of them, were engaging in active Satanic worship of the type described by the Inquisitional writers. Why women were so overwhelmingly singled out has been the cause of much speculation by historians and anthropologists.

Since in large measure, the witch trials were a tool of social control, one theory goes, the members of society who were most vulnerable and least able to fight back were picked on. Indeed, the majority of witches accused in Europe were over fifty. It has also been speculated that many of the women who attracted witchcraft accusations were more independent-minded or "uppity" than was considered desirable by some. Other scholars assert that the witch trials were a particularly virulent expression of an old and deeply ingrained misogyny

Far right: The Witch by David Ryyckaert III, mid seventeenth century. The conjuring of evil spirits and demons was thought to be a common practice of witchcraft

that was allowed to grow in this environment. Whatever the causes, the legacy of the Burning Times has left a scar on both the Catholic and Protestant Churches, and has long served as an example of the worst possible effect of religious and social intolerance.

Those accused in witch trials were typically allowed no defense, and torture was the preferred mode of eliciting the desired confession:

"…the Judge shall use his own persuasions and those of other honest men zealous for the faith to induce her to con⁃ fess the truth voluntarily; and if she will not, let him order the officers to bind her with cords, and apply her to some engine of torture; and then let them obey at once but not joy⁃ fully, rather appearing to be disturbed by their duty." (*Malleus Maleficarum*, Part 3, Question XIV)

Once the confession was extracted, the record of the trial would state that the confession had been made voluntarily. Not only was the confession of guilt for the individual on trial desired—often the accused were further tortured until they gave up the names of their "accomplices" as well. Torture sessions were often deliberately brutal and prolonged, and methods included viselike devices such as thumbscrews and the Spanish boot, which slowly crushed digits or limbs. Stretching the body of the accused on the rack was also a common method, as was burning with hot irons, and most other accepted pain⁃infliction

Above: Sorcerers paying homage to the Devil, from Compendium Malleficarum *by Francesco Guazzo, 1626. Although men were also victims of the witch scares, it is estimated that over 80% of the victims were women.*

The Devil

practices of the time were used at some point during the history of the trials.

There was a range of punishments meted out to the convicted, depending on the severity of their alleged crime. Those only convicted of "light suspicion" might get away with a flogging and short periods of excommunication. More severe punishments included exile or imprisonment and, of course, death. Witches sentenced in the Inquisition were generally executed by burning at the stake, witches found guilty in Protestant courts were usually hanged.

Although the methods used by the Inquisitors (and Protestant tribunals and lay courts) in the stamping out of alleged crimes seem extremely harsh in today's view, we must keep in mind the standards of justice of the time. The Bible is filled with harsh treatment of nonbelievers. As historian Henry Charles Lea describes in his seminal *History of the Inquisition of the Middle Ages* (first edition, 1888):

> "They knew that Christ had said, 'I am not come to destroy the law but to fulfill' (Matthew 5:17). They also knew from Holy Writ that Jehovah was a God delighting in the extermination of his enemies...how Elijah had been commended for slaying four hundred and fifty priests of Baal; and they could not conceive how mercy to those who rejected the true faith could be aught but disobedience to God."

Above: Sorcerers and witches on Sabbath dancing to violin, from Compendium Malleficarum, *by Francesco Guazzo, 1626. Dancing became an activity for which one could be suspected of practicing witchcraft.*

It is the general view of historians that lay people as well as overzealous clergy and prosecutors not only approved of, but desired the meting out of harsh punishments to heretics and witches, for what they considered to be their own protection and the protection of their society and their faith. Many well-meaning people of the time honestly considered it their duty to do whatever they could to help root out heretics and to see to it that they were punished without mercy.

THE RENAISSANCE

In some respects, it hardly seems possible that the same era that ushered in the witch trials also saw the flowering of art and science during the Renaissance. The pre-Renaissance educational mindset of medieval Europe was dominated by the Church. Rather than pushing new areas of inquiry, it was of far greater concern to Rome to establish and promote its ancient authority and thus justify its dominance of religious, moral, and cultural thought. The view of science was largely informed by the writings of Augustine, dating back to before the collapse of the Roman Empire. The Augustinian view held that reason and faith were the means to understand God, but experimental philosophy was evil:

The Alchemist and Death, *from a 1596 manuscript by Abbot Angelo Donati Il Corteggion della Morte. Alchemists worked tirelessly at the elusive goal of turning base metals into gold.*

> "There is also present in the soul, by means of these same bodily senses, a kind of empty longing and curiosity which aims not at taking pleasure in the flesh but at acquiring experience through the flesh, and this empty curiosity is dignified by the names of learning and science."

Left: Saint Michael Overthrowing Satan. *The story of Archangel Michael's defeat of Satan was an extremely popular subject for painters, here attracting the attention of Renaissance master Raphael.*

In this era, with the exception of the sorts of trial and error advances made by working tradesman, artists, and craftsmen in the everyday plying of their trade, the areas of scientific experimentation and exploration largely languished.

Into this rather stagnant atmosphere, the Muslim expansion into Spain in the eleventh century began to open contact with a huge untapped body of learning from an Arab culture that had most definitely not stagnated in the areas of scientific and philosophical thought. The Arab libraries contained a variety of academic treasures. They had copies of great Greek works, which had been thought lost forever in the rubble of the Germanic wreckage of the Roman Empire. Medical texts of Galen and Hippocrates and the complete body of Aristotle's philosophy were just some of the works recovered. Added to these were Oriental ideas and knowledge picked up from the other side of the world, which Europeans had never been exposed to.

One of the areas of study that was introduced to Europe via this Arab conduit was alchemy. In the most simplistic sense, alchemy was the forerunner of modern chemistry. Alchemists, following the Aristotelean idea of the four elements of earth, air, water, and fire, hoped to be able to manipulate the properties of different metals to change one substance into another. Gold, as the purest and most valuable substance known to man, was the ultimate goal of transmutation.

Beyond the well-known stated purpose of trying to affect the transmutation of baser metals into gold, there was also a mystical alchemy at work too: the spiritual transmutation of man into a purer, more perfect version as well. This mystical element to alchemy made its practice somewhat suspect in the minds of some in the Church, who equated it to wizardry. But there were others who attempted to reconcile Christianity with the ideals and purposes of alchemic inquiry, such as Saint Thomas Aquinas.

The introduction of alchemy and its mysteries set the stage for the introduction of one of the most well-known and durable literary characters in western history. Apparently, there was a historical Faust, a German alchemist who contemporaries reported to be well educated and well traveled, but of poor moral reputation. The real Johan Faust reportedly alluded to the Devil as his "Schwager," or crony. The historical Faust died somewhere around 1540.

The Faustus of legend was born of the marriage of this historical figure, Johan Faust, with a type of new traditional folklore that was growing up around tales of Magi—men learned in science and the occult, sometimes called sorcerers or wizards. Variations of these Magi tales got told with the figures of

The Devil

well-known contemporary men such as Roger Bacon or Albertus Magnus substituted in for the generic protagonist.

As his reputation grew, the historical Faust also got inserted into these tales, one collection of which was assembled by an anonymous author and printed under the title *Faustbuch.* The English version, *The History of the Damnable Life and Deserved Death of Doctor John Faustus,* was almost certainly the inspiration for the first well-known version of the Faust legend, playwright Christopher Marlowe's 1588 *Doctor Faustus.*

Doctor Faustus, in his unquenchable desire for universal knowledge (and a little old-fashioned wealth) strikes a deal with the great demon Mephistopheles. In return for 24 years worth of worldly success, Faustus signs over his immortal soul to the Devil.

> Lo, Mephistopheles, for love of thee,
> I cut mine arm, and with my proper blood
> Assure my soul to be great Lucifer's,
> Chief lord and regent of perpetual night!
> View here the blood that trickles from mine arm.
> And let it be propitious for my wish.
> (*Doctor Faustus*, Scene V)

The pact with the Devil signed in blood becomes a popular motif, and soon any arrogant and short-sighted decision made for quick-term benefit and great long-term cost becomes known in the popular lexicon as a Faustian bargain.

Above: Woodcut, 1631, depicting Faustus and Mephistopheles from Christopher Marlowe's Doctor Faustus.

CHAPTER FIVE:

The Romantic Devil

In the aftermath of the Reformation and Renaissance, the culture of Western Europe was irrevocably altered, and with it, the once central and unshakable role of the Church as the dominant force in the everyday life of the people. Historian James Webb concisely characterizes the radical change in his book *The Occult Underground*:

> "From one point of view, what had occurred during the Renaissance/Reformation was roughly this: what might be called the Establishment culture of Western Europe, based entirely upon Christian values as defined by Rome, had at last yielded up its monopoly of jurisdiction—never in theory, of course, but certainly in practice . . . The Renaissance represents the cultural release from the papal straitjacket; the Reformation, the same release expressed in religious terms."

The comparative freedom to explore new scientific, artistic, and philosophical avenues also seemed to create what some historians have termed a variety of "culture shock"—with the blooming interest in alchemy, astrology, and other occult sciencelike pursuits stepping in to serve as a religious substitute for people who were missing the presence of a strong moral/spiritual structure centering their lives.

The post-Renaissance, often called the Age of Reason or the Enlightenment, saw a further weakening of the influence of the Church, particularly among the intellectual and artistic cultural movers and shakers of the time. The popular new idea among eighteenth-century thinkers was deism—a human-centered view, which held that although God did indeed create the universe and everything in it, he then left it to humans to manage and run without further interference. This scientific, progress-focused, here-and-now

Right: Engraving of Flight and Pursuit in Hell *by Gustave Doré, 1861, illustration for Dante's Inferno. Doré's dramatically theatrical renderings were highly suited to the Romantic view of the supernatural.*

perspective pushed the traditional deep concern with the supernatural realm and afterlife underground.

However, this didn't last very long without a reactionary shove back in the other direction. The Age of Reason seemed to leave many people spiritually unsatisfied, questing for something "out there" to help explain and distract us from the mundane and limiting realities of everyday life.

Beginning in the late eighteenth century, a new movement called Romanticism ushered in a different kind of human-centered worldview from the Enlightenment. The Romantics put their focus on emotion, the relationship with nature, and freedom from the scientific and rational constraints of Enlightenment ideals, which they perceived as quashing man's desire for "essential truth."

One of the manifestations of this new Romantic tradition was a resurgence of interest in the occult and supernatural. The Spiritualist movement, sort of a popular cousin to the Romantics, gained popularity through such figures as Emanuel Swedenborg, a former Swedish engineer who claimed to communicate with angels and spirits—perhaps the first celebrated medium. Austrian physician Franz Mesmer introduced the idea of induced trance and wrote the popular volume, *Animal Magnetism* in 1775. Before long, popular "parlor" tricks, such as spirit cabinets, séance, consultations with clairvoyants who could speak with the dead, and tarot card readings, would become fashionable activities for parties and gatherings.

In music, Romanticism found its voice in the compositions of artists such as Ludwig van Beethoven, Frédéric Chopin, and Franz Liszt, who infused their works with intense personal and emotional expressiveness, breaking free of many of the conventions and constraints of the Classical tradition. Here too, themes concentrated on the exotic, original, and often verged into the supernatural.

The Devil tarot card, early twentieth century. Interest in occult and the supernatural, including Tarot, fortune telling, Ouija boards, séance, all blossomed during the Romantic era and continue to be popular today.

Left: The Gates of Hell, *plaster high relief by Auguste Rodin (1840-1917).* The Gates of Hell, *amid depictions of suffering, also features the model for the figure Rodin used for the famous Thinker.*

Art nouveau poster of Pan by Josef Sattler, Germany, 1895/6. Supernatural themes begun in the Romantic era remained fashionable in popular culture on into the 20th century.

It is in the world of literature that the Devil began to get a real Romantic makeover, evolving from the misshapen hair-covered fiend of the Middle Ages, to the misunderstood tragic anti-hero of much Romantic writing.

The first real recasting of Satan as a tragic character prefigured the Romantic movement, but John Milton's 1667 epic poem *Paradise Lost* had a profound impact on literature to follow.

> "Know then, that, after Lucifer from Heaven
> (So call him, brighter once amidst the host
> Of Angels, than that star the stars among)
> Fell with his flaming legions through the deep
> Into his place, and the great Son returned
> Victorious with his Saints, the Omnipotent
> Eternal Father from his throne beheld
> Their multitude, and to his Son thus spake.
> At least our envious Foe hath failed, who thought
> All like himself rebellious, by whose aid
> This inaccessible high strength, the seat
> Of Deity supreme, us dispossessed,
> He trusted to have seized, and into fraud
> Drew many, whom their place knows here no more."
> (*Paradise Lost*, Book 7: 131-144)

Lucifer, as Milton calls Satan before his fall (thus cementing the popular usage of that name for Satan or the Devil) is portrayed throughout *Paradise Lost* as a proud and once-radiant angel, a formerly noble

Right: Engraving of the Mouth of Hell by Dore, 1866. Depiction of fallen angels tumbling into Hell from a scene in John Milton's Paradise Lost.

The Devil

figure brought low by his own arrogance and hubris. But Milton lavishes so much time and attention on fleshing out Satan's character, that the reader almost cannot help but begin to sympathize with his reasoning. It is Satan, rather than the blander representations of God or Adam and Eve that form the center of *Paradise Lost.*

> "Ay me! they little know
> How dearly I abide that boast so vain,
> Under what torments inwardly I groan,
> While they adore me on the throne of Hell.
> With diadem and scepter high advanced,
> The lower still I fall."
> (*Paradise Lost*, Book 4: 86-91)

This is a Satan who bemoans what he has lost, his freedom and will to power. Although Milton himself was a devout Christian, and saw *Paradise Lost* as a triumph for God over Satan, Romantic-era writers reading Milton's work often focused on what they saw as the essential heroism of Satan's struggles against a power greater than himself.

Romantic poets, such as Lord Byron, took up this idea of Satan as a sort of champion of essential truth versus the stultifying limitations of God's plan for humankind. Here, in Byron's poem *Cain*, the "rebellion" Satan is calling for is one of knowledge versus eternal ignorance:

> "I tempt none,
> Save with the truth: was not the Tree, the Tree
> Of Knowledge? and was not the Tree of Life
> Still fruitful? Did I bid her pluck them not?

Right: Engraving of Satan in Council by Gustave Dore, 1866, illustration for Milton's Paradise Lost. Dore was a French painter and illustrator who, although never formally trained, became one of the top book illustrators of the nineteenth century.

The Devil

Did I plant things prohibited within

The reach of beings innocent, and curious

By their own innocence? I would have made ye

Gods; and even He who thrust ye forth, so thrust ye

Because 'ye should not eat the fruits of life,

And become gods as we.' Were those his words?"

French poet and critic Charles Baudelaire has been considered one of the nineteenth-century's greatest talents. A dark, cynical worldview pervaded much of his work. When Baudelaire's first edition of the *Flowers of Evil* collection appeared in 1857, the erotic, lesbian, and Satanic themes resulted in both Baudelaire and his publisher being fined (300 and 200 francs, respectively,) for offending public morality.

"Who but the Devil pulls our walking-strings!

Abominations lure us to their side;

Each day we take another step to hell,

Descending through the stench, unhorrified.

Packed in our brains incestuous as worms

Our demons celebrate in drunken gangs,

And when we breathe, that hollow rasp is Death

Sliding invisibly down into our lungs.

If the dull canvas of our wretched life

Is unembellished with such pretty ware

As knives or poison, pyromania, rape,

It is because our soul's too weak to dare!"

(From "To the Reader," translated by Stanley Kunitz)

Left: Early twentieth-century illustration of Faust and Mephistopheles making their pact from Goethe's (1749–1832) Faust. *Goethe's revisiting of this legend offers a Romantic view of the struggle for knowledge.*

Baudelaire's view of Satan is as a representative of the beauty and power of danger. It is a subversive take, reveling in the rebellion of embracing the darker side of life, the alluring and forbidden thrills that are only possible once standard restrictive morality is abandoned.

With the popularity of this theme of the struggle for knowledge and freedom among Romantic writers, it seems only natural that the Faust legend would be revisited. Goethe's two-part play *Faust* (part one published in 1808, part two published in 1832) is probably the best known. Goethe's version of the story is played out as a microcosm of man's eternal struggle for knowledge and evolution. In this version, as opposed to Marlowe's, Faust's soul is saved. Many critics have explained this as Goethe's attempt to turn Faust's story into an alchemy allegory—a transformation of Faust through his harsh experiences.

Illustration from Olaus Magnus' Historia de Gentibus Septentrionalibus, *1555, showing devils and demons performing manual labor. Devils and demons in folklore often get stuck on the short end of a bargain.*

THE DEVIL IN FOLKLORE

Like Mephistopheles in Goethe's version of Faust, cheated out of the soul he transacted for, the Devil and his minion demons have not fared so well in their bargains as portrayed in popular folklore and legends either. Of course there are plenty of examples of folklore where the Devil is indeed a powerful and malevolent force. These stories often fulfill the role of the cautionary tale, the "be careful what you wish for" variety—such as the story of the father, who, angered by his daughter's frequent complaining mutters a wish that the Devil would take her. Of course the Devil obliges, much to the father's sorrow. But there

Left: Carl Vogel von Vogelstein's Scenes from Faust *by Goethe. The Faust story has been retold many times over the centuries, proving the enduring appeal of its central theme.*

is another current in the folkloric stream, stories dating back even to medieval times, where the demonic characters are portrayed as somewhat slow-witted, and they are often duped or cheated out of their end in a deal.

One old story told of a man who played cards with the Devil. The man, beating the Devil in one hand, won the Devil's planting of "a fine avenue of trees" with the understanding that after the man died, the Devil would be able to claim the man's soul, whether he was buried "inside the church or outside it." The Devil agreed, only to be duped by the man who put a provision in his will to have himself buried in the physical wall of the church, thus voiding the earlier agreement.

It has been argued that the Devil and other demons were portrayed this way as an exercise of desire in the common people to conquer what the Church told them was unconquerable— an expression of resentment at being told that they were perpetually in danger from this crafty and deceptive enemy. Interestingly, most folkloric representations of the Devil are divorced from a specifically religious setting. It almost seems as though Satan's power resides largely within that Christian framework,

Above: Woodcut of the devil appearing to a fever-stricken man, 1843. Although he maintains his recognizably traditional goat-like head, this Devil has affected contemporary dress.

but once removed, he can be treated like any other character.

We begin to see the Devil removed from the religious backdrop more and more as time progresses. References to him in literature often speak of generalized temptation rather than the specific threat of eternal damnation he represents in a more specifically Christian setting. Although there are still plenty of "classic" representations of the demonic figure, complete with horns and a face at least as informed by animal influence as human, we also begin to see a bit more of the Devil incognito.

Once he is no longer so restrained to his religious setting, the Devil begins to pop up more frequently and popularly as an easily recognizable figure who can be used to communicate a great deal in a simple pictorial idea. Political cartoons and editorials often used representations of Satan or demons to convey the notion that the actions of the portrayed parties smack of unholy alliance or an unsavory deal.

Another use of a demonic presence in political or editorial cartoons is the introduction of the notion that sometimes there are ideas so bad, ugly, or distasteful that it doesn't seem possible a person could actually have come up with it of their own free will. This helps us to make sense of unthinkable

Above: Nineteenth-century illustration captioned "Satan's Partner." A demon ponders with a genuinely wicked grin while presiding over warring armies. This depiction still retains some Horned God characteristics.

The Triumvirate.

Three Ministerial Fiends, to-wit
The D--l, Ned Th--rl--o, Billy P--t.
To Rule in H--ll, no Three more fit.
They fram'd the Shop, and Regents Bill,
So fraught with Malice, Spite and Evil,
These precious Ch--nc--l--rs and Devil.
But Reas'n be prais'd, they've staid their furlough,
And each must go, kick'd home by Carlo,
Poor Billy; Belzebub, and Th--rl--o.

Pub.d Jan.y 29.th 1789 by Peter Pindar. London.

events that happen in our lives, especially at the hands of fellow human beings.

One more effect of this process of turning the Devil into a less religiously charged symbol, is his entry into the world of advertising. This 1879 advertisement for the Diebold Safe & Lock Company (overleaf) flexes a little post-apocalyptic humor while demonstrating just what sort of extreme conditions their product can withstand. Presumably, the cheaper competing brand in the background posed no such difficulties for the looting demons.

The Romantic era really marked the close of the classic Devil as a serious and imminent threat outside of some fundamentalist Christian Churches of today. The philosophical and religious take on Satan in the popular mind had been wending for hundreds of years away from belief in the super-demon of the Middle Ages. Satan's continuing hold on us would mostly continue in the folkloric vein, as evidenced by the Devil's many appearances in modern folklore: literature, the stage, and soon, on film.

Above: Satan Tempting Booth to the Murder of the President, *lithograph, c.1865-1867. Satan here is shown in his role as tempter, urging John Wilkes Booth on to the assassination of President Abraham Lincoln.*

Overleaf: This 1879 advertisement depicts the frustration of Satan's minions in being unable to crack a Diebold safe. The Devil begins to appear more often in advertisements as his image becomes less religiously charged.

Left: The Triumvirate, *English engraving, 1789. The decreasing seriousness with which the Devil is feared as a real and physical threat, marks an increase with which his image is used for such purposes as political satire.*

CHAPTER SIX:

The Modern Devil

In the twentieth century and beyond, the specter of Satan and his evil ways has been taken further into the realm of philosophy and popular entertainment. At the same time, various "scares" and "panics" have hit, claiming Satanism is a rampant force invading and pervading youth music and using the new media of movies, television, and the Internet to transmit messages of evil to impressionable young minds.

WHAT IS SATANISM?

What is this concept known as Satanism, and is it for real? Why has it appeared so suddenly at a time when a general belief in Satan as a tangible malevolent force for evil has been in overall decline?

For some extremely conservative or fundamentalist Christians, any person or group who does not believe in a narrowly interpreted Christianity is practicing de facto Satanism. Other people equate Satanism with any of a number of varied occult practices—the occult preoccupation with "secret knowledge" often seems to plant the suspicion that this secret knowledge will be gained with a little unsavory assistance.

In the strictest sense though, Satanism refers to "religious" Satanism, an organized system of beliefs that recognize Satan as a deity, or more often as a "life principle." Much like some of the Romantic poets, religious Satanists believe in a life of rebellion against what they view as constrictive authority (as represented by governments or organized entities such as major religions—particularly Christianity.)

Indeed, it was the nineteenth-century's fascination with everything and anything supernatural or occult that spurred the creation of religious Satanism. One figure who has stirred a lot of controversy, is Aleister

Right: Arch keystone at Brisbane Printing House, Brisbane, Australia, 1910. This whimsical devil is typical of non-threatening grotesque architectural details often used on turn of the nineteenth century buildings.

Crowley, a renowned ceremonial magician and expert in the occult who wrote extensively on the subject. There is no hard evidence that Crowley was in fact a Satanist, although many people who do consider themselves Satanists have read his books.

The foremost proponent of modern Satanism was Anton Szandor LaVey (1930–1997), who founded the Church of Satan in 1966. LaVey's book *The Satanic Bible* is probably the best known and best-selling volume on the subject of religious Satanism. During the counterculture-loving 60s, the Church of Satan garnered a certain amount of publicity. Although the Church of Satan never

Witches Sabbath *(detail), 1819-23. Goya's darkly malevolent, malformed and shadowy women are the sorts of witches nightmares are made of.*

released its membership numbers and it is difficult to gain an accurate census, authorities believe that there are no more than a few thousand people who actually consider themselves practicing Satanists, in spite of widespread rumors of a vast, organized Satanic underground who have been blamed (or credited, depending on one's perspective) with all manner of ritual murder sprees, baby breeding, and the control of segments of multinational corporations and popular entertainment conglomerates.

Persistent rumors about high-level Satanic involvement by the Proctor and Gamble corporation, is the unfortunate result of their old-fashioned corporate logo featuring a crescent moon with stars that some took to be an occult or Satanic symbol.

"Never attribute to Devil-worshipping conspiracies what opportunism, emotional instability, and religious bigotry are sufficient to explain." (Shawn Carlson, Ph.D.)

Another persistent story that has now been classified by most authorities into the "urban legend"

Left: Anton LaVey, founder of the Church of Satan and author of the Satanic Bible *posing in front of a Sigil of Baphomet. LaVey died in 1997 at the age of 67.*

category is the notion of a widespread, worldwide network of Satanic cults that practice what has come to be known as Satanic Ritual Abuse, or SRA. Rumors of people kept locked up in cult homes and abused physically and sexually, both as children and as adults, were given unfortunate legitimacy by several well-known television talk shows in the United States, particularly *The Geraldo Rivera Show.* Rivera, with a background as a news

reporter, appeared to give into the hype of the Satanic Ritual Abuse phenomenon, which authorities now believe to have been an outbreak of attention-seeking individuals. Rivera issued a retraction in 1998, apologizing for having been taken in by the hysteria. After twenty years of rumors and whispering, law enforcement authorities have yet to turn up a single verified case of Satanic Ritual Abuse.

WICCA

Modern witches, practitioners of the Pagan-revival religion Wicca often find themselves correcting misconceptions about their religion and what it does and does not stand for or even recognize. Wicca is a

Above: Medieval Exorcism. In this medieval manuscript drawing from Chartres, a priest is shown driving out the devil. The continued presence of exorcism rites in the Catholic Church is the subject of embarrassment to some modern Catholics.

polytheistic religion, which recognizes divinity in nature and celebrates both the female and male aspects. Due to the long-standing after-effects of the Burning Times, modern witches often find themselves explaining their lack of connection with Satan or Devil worship.

The Devil is a Christian creation, Wiccans point out, and they do not recognize or believe in the divinity of Christ—let alone the trappings and symbols of Christianity. Magic, they insist, has nothing to do with love potions or turning people into toads—with or without demonic assistance. Wiccan magic involves focus of mental and spiritual energy toward a goal, such as peace or healing. The Wiccan code, known as the Rede, states: "An ye harm none, do as ye will"—an ethic that is philosophically opposed to affecting the autonomy of others. In recent years, there has also been a movement to change the stereotypical Halloween costume image of the witch in a pointy hat with disfigured features and multiple horrid warts.

THE DEVIL ON SCREEN

Two old-definition witches (one female, one male) feature heavily in the Devil's major move into modern popular culture, Hollywood-style in Roman Polanski's unnerving 1968 horror classic *Rosemary's Baby*.

Above: Mia Farrow's terrorized young mother who unwittingly births Satan's child in Roman Polanski's chilling 1968 film Rosemary's Baby *haunted an entire generation and ushered in a new breed of horror movie.*

Mia Farrow's Rosemary and her husband move into a new building, never suspecting that her seemingly kindly old neighbors are actually the backbone of a Satan-worshipping group who have arranged to have Old Horny sire Rosemary's baby. The film's paranoid intensity and creepy, only vaguely religious—but certainly recognizable as blasphemous—rituals and chants did as much as anything to plant a notion of religious Satanism in the minds of a mass audience.

The film that really played with some of the more mysterious religious symbolism still present in the Catholic Church was *The Exorcist*. This 1973 film presented indelible images of a very specifically Catholic battle against the forces of evil demons—a battle waged between an evil spirit and a priest through the body of a possessed little girl.

The driving out of spirits was a frequent practice performed by Jesus in the Bible and the techniques of healing and exorcism were reportedly taught by Jesus to his Apostles, so that they could continue his healing work. Clearly, healing and driving out spirits were significant aspects of Jesus' ministry. Throughout the Middle Ages and up to the time that medical science began to explain the presence of many diseases and disorders, exorcisms were a routine practice. However, the fact that exorcism remains "on the books" in the Vatican today is a source of embarrassment to many modern Catholics (they need to apply for permission).

William Friedkin's adaptation of William Peter Blatty's

Left: Linda Blair levitates off her bed in the throes of demonic possession in William Friedkin's 1973 horror classic The Exorcist. *Some film critics still consider it the scariest movie ever made.*

Richard Donner's 1976 film The Omen *helped to introduce the book of Revelation's apocalyptic language (and the number 666) to a mass popular audience.*

frightening novel, *The Exorcist*, delved into what seemed like positively medieval rituals that were housed within the otherwise familiar Church. The battle with the demon who has possessed little Regan is ugly, powerful, and horrible in an old-fashioned Hieronymus Bosch–painting sense—a kind of representation of relentless, putrid evil that had not been portrayed of Satan and his demonic minions in the public consciousness for quite some time.

Linda Blair, the young actress who played Regan, became an instant celebrity following the film's release, but never seemed to satisfy moviegoing audiences to the same degree again in roles that did not require complete revolutions of her demonically made-up head or famous green vomit.

The third movie that really seemed to capture the public's appetite for things devilish was also made in the 70s—Richard Donner's 1976 movie *The Omen*. It has probably called more attention to the prophecies of the book of Revelation than any other single popular culure work. This film, like *The Exorcist* , delves into what are the most fantastic sounding vestiges of ancient beliefs that remain in modern Christian theology. The cataclysmic sounding prophecies—that the Antichrist is among us already and setting into motion the events that signal the end of the world—had a ring for a generation already racked with the worry and dread of growing up in the shadow of the Cold War and nuclear age.

A more recent film version of Satan takes him out of the shadows and suits and places him right

Right: Tim Curry plays a spectacularly art-directed Devil in director Ridley Scott's 1985 film Legend.

The Devil

Members of the Hells Angels motorcycle gang in London, 1971. Dark imagery and attitude became an important component in youth countercul-ture and remains so today.

back into a traditional costume right out of the Middle Ages. Playing opposite Tom Cruise's earnest character of Good, Tim Curry made the devilish Darkness come to life in Ridley Scott's folk tale, *Legend,* made in 1985. Curry's charac-ter boasted outrageously outsized horns, a wicked charm, and skin the color of a bright red chili pepper. Although the movie failed to garner much attention at the box office, Curry's Darkness was a triumph of filmic art direction at the very least.

The Devil has also made many appearances in rock music—well, at least apparently. Since rock and roll first got called the Devil's music back in the 1950s, the popular music their chil-dren listen to has been the source of ire for generations of parents. But it wasn't until the advent of heavy metal rock in the early 70s that a real connection with Satanism began to be made. Groups with names such as Black Sabbath certainly helped get that ball rolling, and other heavy metal groups have cashed in on youth rebellion by throwing a few token mentions of Satan and/or the occult into their lyrics. Led Zeppelin was often cited as a Satanic possibility because of lead guitarist Jimmy Page's well-publicized interest in the writings of magician Aleister Crowley. Modern shock-rocker Marilyn Manson continues the trend.

But the practice—claimed to be Satanic influence—that got the most peculiar interest from the press and public, was the phenomenon known as "backwards masking" or "engineered reversal." Backwards masking involves the alleged planting of certain messages (usually Satanic or occult in nature) that are

Right: John Lovitz as the Devil in a 1986 Saturday Night Live comedy sketch with former NY Yankee's manager Billy Martin. He portrays a ludicrous devil played for laughs, instantly recognizable by visual short-hand—horns, cape, and trident.

only clearly audible when the song is played backwards. Played forwards, these messages are supposedly taken directly into the brain on a subliminal level. Famous accusations of backwards masking appear on such songs as Led Zeppelin's "Stairway to Heaven" where the line "your stairway lies on the whispering wind" is reportedly actually "cause I live with Satan" in reverse.

A much sillier Satan appeared on the long-running television sketch comedy show *Saturday Night Live*—in which comedian John Lovitz donned a Halloween costume devil suit and did his best to menace and threaten (using a weak, ineffective voice and pathetic jabbing gestures with his plastic trident) the show's weekly guest host.

The Devil continues his work as a commercial pitchman, also generally in a nonthreatening vein. The silhouette of the Devil who appears in product placement is most useful for conveying quick messages—in this case, a notion of temperature and a promise that this brand of hot sauce means business.

Above: Lucifer brand hot sauce. There's no quicker visual shorthand to convey heat! The devil's frequent appearances in advertising mark his passage from serious literal threat to beloved folkloric figure.

It is more difficult to find representations of the Devil in the more "serious" art forms today. Nonrepresentational art dominates the museums, and modern notions of Hell often have more to do with remembered Holocaust and future wars than religious ideas about morality and the threat of damnation. Our new Hells are ones of humanity's own making, and we're more apt than our forebears to take all the credit, or rather blame, for creating them. But in spite of his changing and diminished role, it's hard to believe Satan is done with us quite yet.

The figure of the Devil has been with humanity for two millennia now, and he remains one of the most powerful and instantly recognizable symbols in our culture. The idea of an embodiment of sin and temptation is one with seemingly unquenchable appeal. We'll only have to wait and see what Old Horny has in store for us for the next thousand years.

Left: Satan by Georges Roualt, 1933. Modern art's move away from representational images means that twentieth-century paintings of this figure are relatively rare.

Selected Sources and Index

BOOKS

Heaven and Hell in Western Art. Robert
    Hughes. New York: Stein and Day,
    1968

The Satanic Bible. Anton LaVey.
Los Angeles: Feral House, 1989

Devils, Demons and Witchcraft.
Ernst and Johanna Lehner.
New York: Dover Publications, 1972

*Witchcraze: A New History of the European
    Witch Hunts.*
Anne Llewellyn Barstow.
San Francisco: Harper Collins, 1994

The Wonders of the Invisible World.
Cotton Mather and A. Farther.
Wisconsin: Amherst Press, 1862

The Origin of Satan. Elaine Pagels.
New York: Random House, 1999

Sacred Origin of Profound Things. Charles
    Panati.
New York: Penguin USA, 1996

An Encyclopaedia of Occultism. Lewis
Spence.
New York: University Books, 1960

The History of Hell. Alice K. Turner.
Philadelphia: Harvest Books, 1995

The Devil and All His Works. Dennis
    Wheatley. New York: American
    Heritage Press, 1971

The New American Bible. New York:
    Catholic Book Publishing Co., 1970